Chiswick Press

The Literature of Printing

A Catalogue of the Library illustrative of the History and Art of Typography,

Chalcography and Lithography of Richard M. Hoe

Chiswick Press

The Literature of Printing
A Catalogue of the Library illustrative of the History and Art of Typography, Chalcography and Lithography of Richard M. Hoe

ISBN/EAN: 9783337208820

Printed in Europe, USA, Canada, Australia, Japan

Cover: Foto ©ninafisch / pixelio.de

More available books at **www.hansebooks.com**

THE LITERATURE OF PRINTING

A
CATALOGUE
OF THE LIBRARY
ILLUSTRATIVE OF THE HISTORY
AND ART OF TYPOGRAPHY
CHALCOGRAPHY AND
LITHOGRAPHY
OF
RICHARD M. HOE

LONDON PRIVATELY PRINTED
AT THE CHISWICK PRESS
MDCCCLXXVII

 A (C. van der). Iets over de uitvinding en voortgang der Boekdrukkunst. *Utrecht*, 1803, 8vo

ABBOTT (Jacob). The Harper Establishment; or How the Story Books are made. *New York*, 1875, small 4to

ABHANDLUNG von der Buchdruckerkunst, und einigen dahin gehörigen Stücken des Alterthums. *Bremen*, 1740, 8º

ADAMS (Thos. F.). Typographia; or, the Printer's Instructor. A brief sketch of the Origin, Rise and Progress of the Typographic Art, with Practical Directions for conducting every Department in an Office, Hints to Authors, Publishers, etc. *Philadelphia*, 1837, 12mo

ADRY. Catalogue chronologique des imprimeurs et libraires du roy, par le P. ADRY, publié par Le Roux de Lincy. *Paris*, 1849, 8vo *Only fifty copies printed*

[ADRY.] Notice sur les Imprimeurs de la famille des Elzévirs, par un Ancien Bibliothécaire. *Paris*, 1806, 8º

AFFO (Ireneo). Saggio di memorie su la tipografia parmense del secolo XV. *Parma*, 1791, 4to

ALBERT (Andreas). Der Maschinenmeister an der Schnellpresse. Ein Handbuch für Buchdruckereibesitzen. *Leipzig*, 1853, 12mo

ALBUM van Feestliederen en Gezangen, te zingen door de Typographische Vereenigingen, die deel zullen nemen aar de onthullings Feesten, op den 16den Julij, 1856, te Haarlem. *Haarlem*, 1856, small 8º

ALGEMEENE Konst-en Letterbode. *Haarlem*, 1788, etc. 8º *In progress*

ALKEN (Henry). The Art and Practice of Etching; with directions for other methods of light and entertaining Engraving. *London*, 1849, 8vo

ALLAN (George). Life of the late George Allan, Esq. F.S.A., to which is added a Catalogue of Books and Tracts printed at his private Press at Blackwell Grange in the County of Durham. Edited by Robert Henry Allan, Esq. F.S.A. Printed for private use. *Sunderland*, 1829, 8vo
Portrait and plate of arms

ALMELOVEEN (T. Jansen ab). De Vitis Stephanorum celebrium typographorum dissertatio epistolica . . . Subjecta est H. Stephani Querimonia Artis Typographicæ. Ejusdem Epistola de statu suæ Typographiæ. *Amstelædami*, 1683, *small* 8vo

ALNANDER (J. O.). Historiola artis Typographicæ in Suecia. *Rostochi*, 1725, 12mo

ALPHABETE Orientalischer und anderer Sprachen zum gebrauch für Schriftsetzer. *Leipzig*, 1843, 8vo

ALPHABETHS voor Steenhouwers, Schoonschrijvers en Schilders, 2 parts. *Utrecht*, 1860, *oblong* 4to

ALTENBURG. Druckproben der Hofbuchdruckerei in Altenburg. *Altenburg*, 1828, 4to

ALVIN. Les Commencements de la Gravure aux Pays-Bas. Rapport de M. Alvin. *Bruxelles*, 1857, 8º

AMATEUR Printing. Specimens of Amateur Printing. These specimens of Amateur Printing were effected by means of the ingenious little Press invented by Mr. Cowper, and manufactured by Messrs. Holtzapffel and Company. [London] 1840, 4to

AMATI (Giacinto). Ricerche storico-critico-scientifiche sulle origini, scoperte, invenzioni e perfezionamenti fatti nelle arte e nelle scienze, con alcuni tratti biografici della vita dei piu distinti autori nelle medesime. 5 vols. *Milan*, 1818-30, 8º *Notices of Italian Printers contained in vol.* v.

AMBRA (Raffaelle d'). Dei saggi tipografici di Gaetano Nobile nella mostra solenne delle opere di arte ed industria Napolitana. *Napoli*, 1853, 8º

AMERBACH (Joh.). Bibliotheca Amerbachiana. *Basil*, 1659, 4º

AMERICAN Newspaper Reporter and Printer's Gazette. Geo. P. Rowell and Co. Weekly. *New York*, 1867, 8vo   *In progress*

AMERICAN Printer and Lithographer. J. W. Estabrook and Co. Quarterly. *New York*, 1874, 4to
In progress

AMES (Joseph). Typographical Antiquities: being an historical account of Printing in England: with some memoirs of our Antient Printers and a Register of the Books printed by them from the year MCCCCLXXI to the year MDC. With an Appendix concerning Printing in Scotland and Ireland to the same time. *London*, 1749, 4to *Plates*

THE SAME: Begun by the late Joseph Ames, F.R., and A.S.S. and secretary to the Society of Antiquaries. Considerably augmented, both in the Memoirs and Number of Books, by William Herbert. 3 vols. *London*, 1785, 1786, 1790, 4to *The plates are the same as in previous edition*

THE SAME: And now greatly enlarged with copious Notes and illustrated with appropriate Engravings; comprehending the history of English Literature and a View of the Progress of the Art of Engraving in Great Britain; by the Rev. Thomas Frognall Dibdin. 4 vols. *London*, 1810, 1812, 1816, 1819, 4to *plates. Large Paper. Of the large paper of this book only sixty-five copies were printed.*

AMORETTI (Carlo). Lettera sull' anno natalizio d'Aldo Pio Manuzio ed alcune stampe Manuziane, diretta al sig. abate Gaetano Marini. *Roma*, 1804, 8º.

AMPLE PAGE OF KNOWLEDGE, rich with the Spoils of Time, No. 1. Printed by Morison's Patent Ophinine Process. [*London*], 8vo

AMPZING (Samuel). Beschryvinge ende lof der stad Haerlem in rijm bearbeyd, ende met veele oude ende nieuwe stucken buyten Dicht uyt verscheyde Kronijken ... ende diergelijke Schriften verklaerd. Mitsgaders P. Scriverii Laurekranz voor L. Koster, eerste vinder von der boekdruckerye. 2 vols. *Haerlem*, 1628, 4to

AMSTEL (Gebroeders Ploos van). Proef van Letteren, Bloemen, Tekenen, &c. *Amsterdam*, 1767, 8vo

AMSTEL (Ploos van). Beschryving der Letter-gietery. *Amsterdam*, 1790, 4to *2 plates*

ANDENKEN, Gepriesenes, von Erfindung der Buchdruckerey wie solches in Leipzig beym Schluss des dritten Jahrhunderts von den gesammten Buchdruckern daselbst gefeyert worden. *Leipzig*, 1740, 4to

ANDENKEN an das Fest vom 24 Juni als Gedachtnissfeier Gutenbergs und der Erfindung der Buchdruckerkunst. *Lubeck*, 1840, 8vo

ANDREA. Proben aus der Schriftgiesserei der Andreäischen Buchhandlung in Frankfort am Main. 1834, *oblong* 4to

ANFANGSGRUNDE der Buchdruckerkunst. *Leipzig*, 1743, 8º

ANISSON-DUPERRON (E. A. J.). Prémier Mémoire sur l'Impression en Lettres, suivi de la Description d'une nouvelle Presse exécutée pour le service du roi, et publiée par ordre du gouvernement. *Paris*, 1785, 4to

ANNALEN der Typographie, der verwandten künste und gewerbe. Centralorgan für die technischen und materiallen Interessen der Presse. [*Edited by Carl B. Lorck*]. No. 1, July 8, 1869. *Leipzig*, 4to *In progress*

ANNALES Typographiques, rédigées par le Doct. Roux. 10 vols. *Paris*, 1758-1762, 8º

ANNUAIRE de l'Imprimerie et de la Librairie Françaises. *Paris*, 1821, 12º

ANNUAIRE de la librairie, de l'imprimerie, de la papeterie et du commerce de la musique et des estampes. Année 1860. *Paris*, 1860, 8vo *In progress*

ANTONELLI. Biografia del Cav. Giuseppe Antonelli, tipografo. Con rittrato. *Venezia*, 1862, 4º

ANTONUCCI (Gaet. Zaccaria). Catalogo di opere Ebraiche, Greche, Latine, ed Italiane, stampate dai celebri tipografi Soncini nei secoli XV. e XVI. ora per cura di Crescentino Giannini corretto e migliorato. *Fermo*, 1868, 8º

APPLEGATH (A.) and E. Cowper. Description of Applegath and Cowper's Horizontal Machine, and of Applegath's Vertical Machine for Printing "The Times." *London*, 1851, 12º [Extracted from John Weale's " London and its Vicinity."]

ARCHIMOWITZ (T.). Der Papierstereotypie. *Carlsruhe*, 1862, 8º

ARCHIMOWITZ (T.). Neues Franzof stereotyp—verfahren. *Carlsruhe*, 1856-8, 8º

ARCHIV für Buchdruckerkunst und verwandte Geschaftszweige. *Leipzig*, 1865. *In progress*

ARETIN (J. C. A. M. von). Uber die frühesten universalhistorischen Folgen der Erfindung der Buchdruckerkunst . . . mit dem vollständigen Facsimile des ältesten bisher bekannten Teutscher Druckes. *München*, 1808, 4to

ARETIN (J. C. A. M. von). Von den ältesten Denkmählern der Buckdruckerkunst in Baiern, und dem Nutzen ihrer näheren Kenntniss, vorgelesen in einer öffentlichen Versammlung der churf. Akademie der Wissenschaften. *München*, 1801, 4to

ARS MORIENDI. Editio Princeps. Photographisches facsimile des Unicum im besitze von T. O. Weigel in Leipzig. *Leipzig, 1869, folio. In twenty-four leaves, edited with a preface by T. O. Weigel.* 100 *copies only were printed*

ARTE (L') della Stampa, giornale di tipografia, litografia e xilografia. *Firenze*, 1866, 4°
In progress

ASSENSIO Y MEJORADA (Francisco). Geometria de la Letra Romana Majuscula y Minuscula en 28 laminas finas y su Explicacion. *Madrid*, 1780, sm. 4to

ASTLE (Thomas). The Origin and Progress of Writing, as well hieroglyphic as elementary, illustrated by engravings taken from marbles, manuscripts and charters, ancient and modern; also, some account of the origin and progress of printing. *London*, 1784, 4to

ASTLE (Thomas). The Origin and Progress of Writing . . second edition with additions. *London*, 1803, *folio, large paper*, Sir F. Madden's copy

ATKYNS (Richard). The Original and Growth of Printing. Collected out of history and the records of this Kingdome: wherein is also demonstrated that printing appertaineth to the prerogative royal; and is a flower of the crown of England. *London*, 1664, 4°

AUDIFFREDI (J. B.). Letere Tipografiche dell' Abate N. Ugolini. 1778, 8°

AUER (Alois). Album der k. k. Hof-und Staats-Druckerei in Wien. Die Vereinigung der graphischen Kunste. 4 vols. *Wien*, 1850-53, *folio*

AUER (A.). Discovery of the Natural Printing Process. [In German, English, Italian, and French.] *Wien*, 1854, *folio*. 20 *plates of the Nature Printing Process and* 6 *pages of fac-simile of Henry Bradbury, who claimed priority in the invention*

AUER (A.). Geschichte der K. K. Hof-und Staats-Druckerei in Wien, von einem Typographen dieser anstalt. A History of the Imperial and Government Printing Establishment at Vienna, by one of its members. *Wien*, 1851, 8vo

Auer (A.). Der Polygraphische Apparat, oder die verschiedenen Kunstfächer der kk. Hof-und Staatsdruckerei zu Wien. *Wien*, 1853, 8*vo*

Auer (A.). The Polygraphic Apparatus, or the different departments of art carried on in the Imperial Court and Government Printing Office at Vienna. *Vienna*, 1853, 8*vo*

Auer (A.). Ueber das Raumverhältniss der Buchstaben [pp. 51 *to* 112 *of the Transactions of the Vienna Academy*, 1850], 4*to*

Author's Assistant (the) to Printing and Publishing. *London*, 1840, 12º

Bachelier. Spécimen de l'Imprimerie de. *Paris*, 1849, 4*to*

Bachmann (J. H.). Neues Handbuch der Buchdruckerkunst. *Weimar*, 1876, *cr*. 8*vo*

Bachmann (J. H.). Die Schriftgieszerei. *Leipzig*, 1868, 4*to*

Bachmann (J. H.). Die Schule des Musiknoten-Satzes. *Leipzig*, 1865, 4*to*

Bachmann (J. H.). Die Schule des Schriftsetzers. *Braunschweig*, 1858-9, 8º

Baer (F. C.). Lettre sur l'Origine de l'Imprimerie. *Strasbourg (Paris)*, 1761, 8º

Bagford (John). An Essay on The Invention of Printing; with an account of Mr. Bagford's Collections for the same. 1705, 4º [Philosophical Transactions Abridged, vol. **xxv.**]

Baille (Lodovico). Vicende tipografiche di Sardegna. *Cagliari*, 1847, 8º

Baker (Peter C.). Franklin; An address delivered before the New York Typographical Society, on Franklin's Birthday, Jan. 12, 1865. *New York*, 1865, 8*vo*

Baldinucci (Filippo). Cominciamento e progresso dell' arte di intagliare in rame, colle vite di molti de' più eccellenti maestri della stessa professione. *Milano*, 1808, 8*vo*. *Forming vol*. 1 *of the works of Baldinucci*, **14** *vols*.

BALL (William). A Briefe Treatise concerning the regulating of Printing, humbly presented to the Parliament of England. *London*, 1651, 12º

BALLERSTEDT (G.). Vollständiges Handbuch der Steindruckerei. *Quedlinburg*, 1837, 8º

BALLHORN (Fried.). Alphabete Orientalischer und Occidentalischer Sprachen zum gebrauch für Schriftzetser und Correctoren. *Leipzig*, 1856, 8vo

BANCELIN-DUTERTRE (Charles). Annuaire des Imprimeurs et des Libraires. *Paris*, 1829, 12mo

BANDINI (Angelo Maria). De Florentina Juntarum Typographiâ ejusque censoribus ex qua Græci, Latini, Turci scriptoris ope codicum manuscriptorum a viris clarissimus pristinæ integritati restituti in lucem prodierunt. Accedunt excerpta uberrima præfationum libris singulis præmissarum. *2 parts. Lucæ*, 1791, 8vo

BANDTKIE (J. S.). De Primis Cracoviæ in arte Typographica Incunabulis. *Cracoviæ*, 1812, 4to

BANDTKIE (J. S.). Historya Drukarú Krakowskisch. *Krakowie*, 1815, 8º

BANDTKIE (J. S.). Historya Drukarú w królestwie Polskiem i Wielkiem Xiestwie Litewskiem, 3 vols. *Krakowie*, 1826, 8º

BANKES (H.). Lithography; or the Art of Making Drawings on Stone, for the purpose of being multiplied by Printing. *London*, 1813, 8º

BARBERA (Piero). Ricordi biografici di Vincenzo Batelli, tipografo Fiorentino. *Firenze*, 1872, 8º

BARTOLINI (Antonio). Saggio Epistolare sopra la Tipografia del Friuli nel secolo XV. aggiuntavi una lettera Tipografica del signor abbate J. Morelli. *Udine*, 1798, 4to

BARUFFALDI (Girolamo). Della Tipografia Ferrarese dall' anno 1471 al 1500. *Firenze*, 1777, 8º

BASCHET (Armand). Aldo Manuzio. Lettres et Documents, 1495-1515. *Venetiis*, 1867, 8º 160 copies printed. Not for sale

BASKERVILLE (John). *A life of this celebrated Birmingham printer is in preparation by Mr. Samuel Timmins. See Notes and Queries, June 10,* 1876

BATE (John). The Mysteries of Nature and Art. In foure severall parts. The first of Water Works. The second of Fireworks. The third of Drawing,

Washing, Limming, Painting and Engraving. The fourth of Sundry Experiments. *London*, 1635, 4º

BAUDOUIN (P. A.). Anecdotes historiques du temps de la Restauration, suivies de recherches sur l'origine de la presse. *Paris*, 1853, 8vo

BAUER (E. C.). Primitiæ Typographiæ Spirenses, oder Nachrichten von der ersten und berühmten Drachischen Buchdruckerey in der Reichs-Stadt Speyer und denen in dem XV^ten bis zu anfang des XVI^ten Seculi daselbst gedruckten merckwürdigen Büchern. Wie auch dem ersten und raren Speyrischen Neuen Testament. *Speyer*, 1764, sm. 8º

BAUMGARTEN-CRUSIUS (L. F. O.). Festrede bei der akademischen Secularfeier von der erfindung der Buchdruckerkunst zu Jena. *Jena*, 1840, 8vo

BAUTZ (J. B. B.). Die Lithographie in ihrem ganzen Umfange. *Augsburg*, 1836, 8º

[BAVEREL (J. P.) et MALPEZ]. Notices sur les Graveurs qui nous ont laissé des Estampes marquées de Monogrammes, Chiffres, Rébus, Lettres Initiales, etc. avec une description de leurs plus beaux ouvrages et des Planches en taille-douce, contenant toutes les marques dont ils se sont servis; suivies d'une Table qui en donne explication. 2 vols. *Besançon*, 1807, 8vo

BEADNELL (Henry). Guide to Typography, Literary and Practical, or the Reader's Handbook and the Compositor's Vademecum. 2 parts. *London*, 1859, *crown 8vo*

BEAUPRÉ (M.). Recherches historiques et bibliographiques sur les commencements de l'Imprimerie en Lorraine, et sur ses progrès jusqu'à la fin du XVII. siècle. *St.-Nicolas-De-Port*, 1845, 8vo

BECKER (Carl). Jost Amman, Zeichner und Formschneider, Kupferätzer und Stecher. Nebst Zusätzen von R. Weigel. *Leipzig*, 1854, 4º 17 *woodcuts*

BECKER (F. P.). Specimens of Engraving by the Omnigraph. *London*, [1850], 4to

BEICHLINGEN (Zachaire á). Fons Bibliothecarum inæstimabilis; das ist, wahrer Unterricht von Ursprung, &c. der Buchdruckereyen, &c. *Eisleben*, 1699, 4º

[BELINFANTE (J. J.)]. Lourens Janszoon Coster, uitvinder der Boekdrukkunst, te Haarlem, omstreeks 1423. Oprigting van het standbeeld tot Coster's eere, der stad Haarlem aangeboden als hulde van Neerlands volk. *Amsterdam*, no date (about 1820), 4to

BELLERMANN (C.). Δῶρον Βασιλικόν, oder das mehr als Konigliche, ja Göttliche Geschencke der Buchdruckerey, &c. *Erfurt*, 1740, 8º

BENIOWSKI (Major). Improvements in Printing. *London*, 1854, 12mo

BENSLEY (B.). Specimens of Types. *Woking*, 1842, 8vo

BERARD (A. S. L.). Essai Bibliographique sur les Editions des Elzévirs les plus précieuses et les plus recherchées. *Paris*, 1822, 8vo

BERGELLANUS (Joannes Arnoldus). De Chalcographiæ Inventione, poema encomiasticum. *Moguntiæ*, 1541, 4º

BERJEAU (J. P.). Catalogue Illustré des Livres Xylographiques. *Londres*, 1865, 8vo Only 105 copies printed

BERJEAU (J. P.). Early Dutch, German, and English Printers' Marks. *London*, 1866, 8vo

BERJEAU (J. P.). Speculum Humanæ Salvationis: reproduit en facsimile, avec Introduction, Historique et Bibliographique. *Londres*, 1861, 4to

BERNARD (Auguste Joseph). Antoine Vitré et les Caractères orientaux de la Bible Polyglotte de Paris. *Paris*, 1857, 8º

BERNARD (A. J.). Archéologie Typographique. *Bruxelles*, 1853, 8vo 100 copies printed separately, from the Bulletin du Bibliophile Belge, tome 1er 2e serie

BERNARD (A. J.). De l'Origine et des Débuts de l'Imprimerie en Europe. 2 vols. *Paris*, 1853, 8vo

BERNARD (A. J.). Geofroy Tory, peintre et graveur, premier imprimeur royal, réformateur de l'orthographe et de l'imprimerie sous François Ier, Deuxième édition, entièrement refondue. *Paris*, 1865, royal 8vo Large paper

BERNARD (A. J.). Histoire de l'Imprimerie Royale du Louvre. *Paris*, 1867, royal 8vo

BERNARD (A. J.). Historique de la Proposition du Congrès Typographique. [*Paris*, 1855], 8º

BERNARD (A. J.). Les Estiennes. [*Extract from Didot, Biographie Générale.*] 8vo

BERNARD (A. J.). Les Estienne et les Types Grecs de François 1er, complément des annales Stéphaniennes, renfermant l'histoire complète des types royaux, enrichie d'un specimen de ces caractères et suivie d'une notice historique sur les premières impressions grecques. *Paris*, 1856, 8vo

BERNARD (A. J.). Notice Historique sur l'Imprimerie Nationale. *Paris*, 1848, 32º

BERNARDI (Jacopo). Vita di Giambattista Bodoni. *Saluzzo*, 1872, 8º

BERNARDI (Jacopo), ZENGHELLINI (Antonio), e VALSECCHI (Antonio). Intorno a Panfilo Castaldi da Feltre e alla invenzione di caratteri mobili per la stampa, memoria e dissertazioni. *Milano*, 1866, 4to

BERNER (F.). Der Druckerei in ihrem ganzen Umfange. 2 vols. *Stuttgart*, 1853, 16º

BERNHART (J. B.). Das Druckjahres der Kosmographie der Ptolemaeus 1462; Namen der Buchdrucker des Joannis de Turrecremata explanatio in Psalterium Cracis impressa. Schreiberzüge im Theuerdank von 1517. Kennzeichen und Alter von Guttenberg und Faust in Mainz gedruckten lateinischen Bibel. (*München*, 1804-5), 8vo

BERNHART (Mathias). Geschichte der Entstehung, Ausbildung und Verbreitung der Buchdruckerkunst. *München*, 1807, 8vo

BERTHIAUD. Nouveau Manuel Complet de l'Imprimeur en taille douce. *Paris*, 1837, 12mo

BERTRAND QUINQUET. Traité de l'Imprimerie. *Paris*, an vii. (1798), 4to

BESLEY (R.). General Specimen of Printing Types. *London*, 1847, 4to

BESLEY (R.). Supplementary Sheets. *London*, 1848, 4to

BESLEY and Co. (R.) New Specimens of Mathematical Combination Borders and other Typographical Ornaments. *London*, 4º

BESNARD (J.). Epreuves des Vignettes et Fleurons polytypes, gravés sur cuivre en tailles de relief à l'usage de l'imprimerie. *Paris*, 1812, fº

BESOLDI (Christ.). Dissertationum Philologicarum .... III. De Inventione Typographiæ. *Tubingæ*, 1620, 4to

BETTONI (Nicolo). Lettere Tipografiche da Milano. *Milano*, 1821, 8º

Bettoni (N.). Memorie Biografiche di un tipografo Italiano. *Parigi, 1836, 8º The continuation bears the following title:*—Mémoires biographiques d'un typographe Italien. *Paris,* 1845, 8º

Bettoni (N.). Saggio di guerra tipografico, lettera alla vedova Pomba. *Milano,* 1820, 8º

Beughem (Corn. à.). Incunabula Typographiæ. *Amsterdam,* 1688, 12º

Beyer (C.). Praktische Handbuchlein der Steindruckerei. *München,* 1863, 16º *7 plates*

Beyschlag (D. E.). Beyträge zur Kunstgeschichte der Reichsstadt Nördlingen, &c. *Nördlingen,* 1798-99, 8º

Bianchi (Isidoro). Sulle Tipografie Ebraiche di Cremona nel secolo XVI. Col ragguaglio di un Salterio Ebraico stampato in detta citta nel secolo medesimo. Dissertazione storico-critica. *Cremona,* 1807, 8vo

Biblia. Aurea Biblia Vetus et Novi Testamenti. *Printed in black letter, the initials, etc. filled in with red, blue, and green inks. Ulmæ, J. Zeiner de Reutlingen,* 1476, *folio*

Biblia Pauperum, nach dem original in der Lyceumsbibliothek zu Constanz, herausgegeben von Laib und Schwarz. *Zurich,* 1867, *folio*

Biblia Pauperum. Beschrijving van een nieuwlings ontdekt exemplaar van de Biblia Pauperum en de Ars Moriendi. *Amsterdam,* 1839, 8vo

Bidwell (G. H.). Treatise on the Imposition of Forms. *New York,* 1866, 12mo

Bibliophile Belge. Bulletin du Bibliophile Belge (by MM. de Reiffenberg, Chenedollé, A. Scheler, etc.). *Bruxelles,* 1845-65, 21 vol., table des tom. I. à X., et Annales Plantiniennes, together 23 vols.—Le Bibliophile Belge. Nouvelle série (by the Société des Bibliophiles Belges.). Vols. 1 to 10. *Bruxelles,* 1866-75, 8vo

Bignan (A.). Epitre à quelques ennemis des Lumières, sur la Découverte de l'Imprimerie, qui a obtenu l'*Accessit* au Jugement de l'Académie Française, dans la Séance publique du 25 Août, 1829. *Paris,* 1829, 8º

Binder (E.), and C. Rohlacher. Der Steinüberdruck. *Meiningen,* 1851, 4º

Binger (M. H.). Glyphographie uit het Etablissement van M. H. Binger. *Amsterdam,* 4to *Numerous illustrations*

BLADES (William). How to tell a Caxton, with some hints where and how the same might be found. *London*, 1870, 8º

BLADES (W.). The Life and Typography of William Caxton, England's first printer; with evidence of his typographical connection with Colard Mansion, the printer, at Bruges. 2 vols. *London*, 1861, 4to *With plates*

BLADES (W.). A list of medals, jettons, tokens, &c. in Connection with Printers, and the Art of Printing. *London*, 1866, *fcap*. 4to *Only 25 copies printed*

BLANSCH (H. le). Beknopte en volledige Handleiding tot het overslaan van Drukvormen. *s'Gravenh*. 1844, *oblong 8vo*

BLEEKRODE (S.). De Tentoonstelling te Londen. [*Long account of printing machines, &c. at the Exhibition of* 1851.] *s'Gravenhage*, 1853, 8vo

BLEEKRODE (S.). Het Bankbillet. De Kunstbewerkingen en de Waarborgen voor zijne echtheid, volgens A. Smee en H. Bradbury behandeld. [1856] 8º *two plates of specimen notes and one of bank-note printing machine*

BLIND. Dritte [und Vierde] Onderricht, Leer en Leesboek. 2 parts, 1808, *sm*. 4to *Printed in embossed type*

BLON (J. C. le). L'Art d'imprimer les Tableaux. Traité d'après les Ecrits, les Opérations et les Instructions verbales de J. C. le Blon. Seconde édition. *Paris*, 1768, 8º

BLUMENFELD (J. C.). Die drei Tage Gutenbergs in Strassburg. *Strassburg*, 1840, 12mo

BOCKENHOFFER (Joh. Phil.). Exempla Literarum Typographicarum, quæ reperiuntur in Regiæ Majestatis et Academiæ Hafniensis Typographia, &c. *Hafnæ*, 1691, *f*º

BODEMANN (Eduard). Xylographische und Typographische Incunabeln der königlichen öffentlichen Bibliothek zu Hannover ... mit 41 Platten typographischer Nachbildungen der Holzschnitte und Typenarten .... und 16 Platten mit den Wasserzeichen des Papiers. *Hannover*, 1866, 4to

BODONI (Giambattista). Iscrizioni esotiche a Caratteri novellamente incisi e fusi [for the Baptism of Ludovico, Prince of Parma.] *Parma*, 1774, 4to

BODONI. Manuale Tipografico, 2 vols. *Parma*, 1818, *royal* 4to

BODONI. Medaglie d'onore decretata dal pubblico di Parma al celebre **tipografo** G. B. Bodoni. *Parma*, 1806, *f°*

BODONI. Memorie aneddote per servire un giorno alla vita del signor Giovanbattista Bodoni, tipografo di sua Maestà Cattolica e direttore del Parmense tipografeo. *Parma*, 1804, *8vo*

BODONI. Vita del Cavaliere Giambattista Bodoni, Tipografo Italiano, e Catalogo cronologico delle sue Edizioni. [by G. de Lama.] **2** vols. *Parma*, 1816, *small 4to*

BODONI : BULMER. **A** specimen of printing, 2 leaves 4to by Bulmer, intended **to show** the equality **of** his press to that of Bodoni

BOHN (Henry George). The Origin and Progress of Printing. A Lecture delivered at Twickenham, April 8th, and repeated by desire at Richmond, April 21st, 1857. *London*, 1857, *8vo Privately printed for the members of the Philobiblon Society*

BOITEAU D'AMBLY (Paul). Produits de l'Imprimerie et **de la** Librairie [Exposition Universelle de 1867]. *Paris*, 1867, *8vo*

BONI (M.). Lettere sui primi libri **a** stampa di **alcuni** città e terre dell' Italia superiore, parte sinora sconosciuti, parte nuovamente illustrati. *Venezia*, **1794, 4to**

BONNARDOT (Alf.). Histoire artistique et archéologique de la Gravure **en** France. *Paris*, 1849, royal 8° *Only three hundred copies printed.*

BONNÉ (D.). Het Boekdrukken, boertende zamenspraak, **met** Zang tusschen Klaas, een Zetter en Jan, een Drukker. Ter Eere van den Uitvinder dier Kunst Laurens **Janszoon** Koster. [*Dordrecht*, 1823], *8vo*

BOOKWORM. The Bookworm, an illustrated Literary **and** Bibliographical Review. [Edited by J. Ph. Berjeau]. 5 vols. *London*, 1866-70, *8vo. With facsimiles of printer's marks, etc.*

BOOTH (Joseph). An Address to the Public on the Polygraphic Art invented by Mr. Joseph Booth, Portrait Painter. **London,** 1788, 8°

BORAO (Géronimo). La Imprenta en Zaragoza, con **noticias** preliminares sobre **la** Imprenta en general. *Zaragoza*, 1860, *8vo*

BORIES (J.) and BONASSIES (F.). Dictionnaire pratique de **la presse**, de l'imprimerie et de la librairie, suivi d'un code complet contenant les lois, ordonnances etc. sur la matiere. 2 vols. *Paris*, 1847, 8*vo*

BORSTIUS (Gerard). Oratio de Typographiæ Laudibus. *Amstel.* 1728, 4*to*

BONY (J. T.). Les Origines de l'Imprimerie à Marseille, Recherches Historiques et Bibliographiques. *Marseille*, 1858, 8° *Only 100 copies printed*

BOSSCH (Herman). Memoria Hieronymi de Bosch rite celebrata a D. J. van Lennep, et Carmen de Inventæ Typographiæ Laude Kostero Harlemensi potenter tandem asserta: auctore Hermanno Bosscha. *Amstelodam*, 1817, 4*to*

BOSSE (Abraham). Traicté des manières de Graver en taille-douce sur l'airain, par le moyen des eaues fortes et des vernix durs et mols; ensemble de la façon d'en imprimer les planches et d'en construire la presse et autres choses concernant les dits arts. *Paris*, 1645, 8° *Plates*

BOSSE (A.). Tractaet in wat Manieren men op Root Koper Snijden ofte Etzen zal: door de Middel der Stercke-Wateren, ende Harde-en Zachte-Vernissen, ofte Gronde: als mede de Manieren der zelve Plaeten te Drucken, de Pars te maecken, ende andere dinghen, behelzende de zelve Konsten. In 't Fransch beschreven, In 't Nederduyts overgezet door P. H. *Amsterdam*, 1662, 12°

BOSSE (A.). De la Manière de graver à l'eau-forte et au burin, et de la gravure en manière noire. *Paris*, 1745, 8*vo*

BOUBERS (J. L. DE). Epreuves des Caractères de la Fonderie de. *Bruxelles*, 1777, 8*vo*

BOULARD (M. S.). Le Manuel de l'Imprimeur, ouvrage utile à tous ceux qui veulent connoître les détails des ustensiles, des prix, de la manutention de cet Art intéressant, & à quiconque veut lever une Imprimerie. *Paris*, 1791, 8*vo*

BOULMIER (Joseph). Etudes sur le Seizième Siècle. Estienne Dolet, sa vie, ses œuvres, son martyre. *Paris*, 1857, 8*vo*

BOUTMY (Eugène). Les Typographes Parisiens, suivis d'un petit dictionnaire de la Langue Verte Typographique. *Paris*, 1874, 8*vo*

BOUTON (V. M.). Traité Elémentaire et Pratique pour apprendre à graver sans maître. *Paris, crown* 8*vo*

Bowyer (William). The Original of Printing, in two Essays. 1. The substance of Dr. Middleton's Dissertations on the Origin of Printing in England; 2. Mr. Meerman's Account of the Invention of the Art at Haerlem and the Progress to Mentz, with occasional remarks and an Appendix. *London*, 1774, 8vo Second edition, enlarged. *London*, 1776, 8vo Supplement by Nichols, 1781, 8vo

Boxhornii (Marci Zuerii). De Typographicæ Artis Inventione et Inventoribus, dissertatio. *Lugd. Bat.* 1640, 4to

Bozzo (G.). Della Stamperia della Regia Università di Palermo. *Palermo*, 1850, 8°

Bradbury (Henry). Lecture on Natural Printing, at the Royal Institution, May 11, 1855. *London*, 1856, 8°

Bradbury (H.). On the Security and Manufacture of Bank Notes. A Lecture as delivered at the Royal Institution of Great Britain, Albemarle Street, Friday evening, May 9, 1856. *London*, 1856, 4to 2 plates

Bradbury (H.). Printing, its Dawn, Day and Destiny. *London*, 1858, 4to

Bradshaw (Henry). List of the founts of type and woodcut devices used by Printers in Holland in the fifteenth century. *London*, 1871, 8°

Branca (Carlo). Abbozzo bibliografici di un vecchio librajo. *Milano*, 1866, 4°

Branca (C.). Catalogo della sua libreria, preceduto da brevi cenni bibliografici. *Milano*, 1844, 8°

Brandenburgh (H.). Letterproef der Boekdrukkerij. *Workum*, 1828, sm. f°

Brandolese (Pietro). La Tipografia Perugina del secolo XV., illustrata del Signor Vermiglioli e presa in esame. *Padova*, 1807, 8°

Braun (Placidus). Notitia historico-litteraria de libris ab artis typographicæ inventione usque ad annum 1479 impressis in bibliotheca liberi, ac Imperialis monasterii ad SS. Udalricum et Afram Augustæ, extantibus. *Augustæ Vindelicorum*, 1788, 4to

Brede (C. L.). Einige Schriftproben nebst verzierungen. *Offenbach* [1828], 8vo

Brégeaut (L. R.). Manuel complet, théorique et pratique, du Dessinateur et de l'Imprimeur-Lithographe. Troisième édition. *Troyes*, 1834, 18°

BRÉGEAUT (L. R.) Nouveau Manuel Complet de l'Imprimeur Lithographe. *Paris*, 1850, 12*mo*

BREHMEN (C.). Gründliche Bericht von Erfindung der Buchdruckereykunst, &c. *Dresden*, 1640, 4°

BREITKOPF (J. G. I.). Beschreibung des Reichs der Liebe, mit beygefügter Landcharte. Ein zweyter Versuch im Satz und Druck geographischer Charters, durch die Buchdruckerkunst. *Leipzig*, 1777, 4°

BREITKOPF (J. G. I.). Exemplum Typographiæ Sinicis figuris characterum e typis mobilibus compositum. *Lipsiæ*, 1789, 4°

BREITKOPF (J. G. I.). Nachricht von der Stempelschneiderei und Schriftgiesserei. *Leipzig*, 1777, 4°

BREITKOPF (J. G. I.). Ueber den Druck der geographischen Charten: nebst beygefügter probe einer durch die Buchdruckerkunst gesetzen und gedruckten Landcharte. *Leipzig*, 1777, 4°

BREITKOPF (J. G. I.). Ueber die Geschichte der Enfindung der Buchdruckerkunst. *Leipzig*, 1779, 4*to*

BREITKOPF (J. G. I.). Versuch, den Ursprung der Spielkarten, die Einführung des Leinenpapieres, und den Anfang der Holzschneidekunst in Europa zu erforsehen. *Leipzig*, 1784, 4*to*—Theil 2. Beyträge zu einer Geschichte der Schreibekunst der Schönschreibekunst und der Kinder der Zeichenkunst, Bildschnitzerey, Mahlerey und Musaik ... nebst einer Geschichte der Mahlerey in den Handschriften u. s. w. von J. G. I. Breitkopf. Aus des Verfassers nachlasse herausgegeben und mit einer Vorrede begleitet von J. C. F. Roch. *Leipzig*, 1801, 4*to*

BRIGHTLY (Charles). The Method of Founding Stereotype, as practised by Charles Brightly of Bungay, Suffolk. *Bungay*, 1809, 8°

BRILL (E. J.). Het gehed des Heeren, in veertien talen. Strekkende tot Proeve van Letters, van het gewoon Europeesch karakter afwijkende. *Leiden*, 1855, 4*to*

BRILL (E. J.). Proeve van Letteren der Boekdrukkerij van E. J. Brill te Leiden. 1859, 8*vo*

BRISSART-BINET (Ch.). Cazin marchand libraire Rémois ... Sa vie et ses éditions. *Bruxelles*, 1860, 8°

BROECKX (C.). Lettre à M. le Docteur P. J. van Meerbeeck de Malines sur une publication de

R. Dodoens, inconnue des Bibliophiles. *Anvers,* 1862, 8*vo*

BROECKX (C.). Notice sur un livre de médecine prétenduement imprimé en 1401. *Anvers,* 1847, 8*vo*

BRŒNNER (H. L.). Proben der neuen Antiqua, Cursiv und Fraktur Schriften. *Frankfurt,* 1826, 8*vo*

BROFFERIO (Angelo). Cenni Storici intorno all' Arte Tipografica e suoi progressi in Piemonte, dall' invenzione della Stampa sino al 1835. *Milano,* 1876, 8*vo*

BROGIOTTUS (**Andrea**). **Indice de' Carratteri con l'inventori e nomi di essi esistenti nella Stampa Vaticana e Camerale.** *Roma,* 1628, 8*vo*

BROU (**Ch. de**). La Chronique de Godefroid de Bouillon (*printed about* 1486). *Bruxelles,* 1865, 8*vo*

BROU (Ch. de). Marques d'imprimeurs. [*Bruxelles,* 1850] 8*vo Woodcuts of printers' marks. Only 25 copies printed from the "Bulletin du Bibliophile Belge"*

BROU (**Ch. de**). Quelques **mots** sur **la** gravure **au** Millésime de 1418. *Bruxelles,* 1846, 4*to,* **7 *plates***

BRUCKNER (G.). Geschichte der Enfindung der Buchdruckerkunst. *Schleusingen,* 1840, 8º

BRUN (Marcelin). Manuel Pratique et Abrégé de la Typographie Française. *Paris,* 1825, 12*mo* Second edition. *Bruxelles,* 1826, 12*mo*

BRUNET (**Pierre Gustave**). Imprimeurs imaginaires et libraires supposés. Etude bibliographique, **suivie de recherches sur** quelques ouvrages imprimés avec des indications fictives de lieux, **ou** avec **des** dates singulières. *Paris,* 1866, 8*vo*

BRUYN (Hendrik) en Comp. Verbeterde Letterproef **waar in** verscheide nieuwe Schriften. *Amsterdam,* 8*vo*

BUCHDRUCKER (der), ein Wochenblatt. Von J. L. Schwatz, &c. *Hamburg,* 1766 and 1775, 8º

BUCHDRUCKERKUNST und Schriftgiesserey, mit ihren Schriften, Formaten und allen dazu gehörigen Instrumenten abgebildet auch klärlich beschrieben. Mit eine Vorrede von J. E. Kappens. 2 vols. *Leipzig,* 1740, 8º

BUCHDRUCKZEICHNUNG (die), oder Glyphographie. *Leipzig,* 1846, 8º

BUCHER und BLATTER. Monatschrift für die Pressgewerbe. *Darmstadt,* 1870, 4º *In Progress*

BUFFALO SPECIMEN (The). *Chicago,* 1867, 4*to*
  In Progress

BULLET (J. B.). Recherches Historiques sur les Cartes à jouer, avec des Notes Critiques. *Lyon*, 1757, 8°

BUNEMANN (Joseph Lewis). Notitia Scriptorum editorum atque ineditorum Artem Typographicum illustrantium intermixtis passim Observationibus literariis ordine alphabetico in memoriam Saeculi Tertii ab inventa Typographia decursi occasione Actus oratorii a sedecim juvenibus lectissimis anno 1740 die Maii decima. Habendi exhibit ac summos atque optimos quosque Patronos et Fautores ed eos benevole audiendos devotissime invitat. *Hanoveræ*, 1740, 4°

BURBURE (Léon de). Sur l'Ancienneté de l'Art Typographique en Belgique, 8° *Extract from the Bulletin de l'Académie Royale de Belgique*

BURDICK (W.). An Oration on the nature and effects of the Art of Printing, delivered in Franklin Hall, July 5, 1802, before the Boston Franklin Association. *Boston [U.S.]* 1802, 8vo

BURE (G. F. de). Museum Typographicum, seu Collectio in qua omnes fere libri in quavis facultate ac Lingua rarissimi notatuque dignissimi accurate recensentur. *Paris*, 1755, 12° *Twelve copies only printed for private distribution. Reprinted 1775*

BURGES (Francis). Some Observations on the Use and Original of the Noble Art and Mystery of Printing. *Norwich*, 1701, 8°

BYLAERT (Jean Jacques). Nouvelle manière de graver en cuivre des estampes coloriées; de façon que, quoique imprimées dans une presse ordinaire, elles conserveront l'air et le caractère du dessin. Traduit du Hollandais par L. G. F. Kerroux. *Leyde*, 1772, 8°

(R. M.). Almanach de l'Imprimerie et de la Librairie pour 1819. *Paris*, 1819, 8vo

CABALLERO (Raymundo Diosdado). De Prima Typographiæ Hispanicæ ætate Specimen. *Romæ*, 1793, 4°

CABALLERO (Raymundo Diosdado). De Prima Typographiæ Hispanicæ ætate Specimen. Breve examen acerca de los primeros tiempos del Arte Tipografico en España, version Castellana por D. Vicente Fontan. *Madrid*, 1866, 8vo

CABRERA NUNEZ DE GUZMAN (Melchor de). Discurso legal, historico y politico en prueba del Origen, Progressos, Utilidad del Arte de la Imprenta. *Madrid*, 1675, f°

CAMBIAGI (Francesco). Cenni storici della Stamperia granducale. *Firenze*, 1846, 4°

CAMPBELL (M. F. A. G.). Annales de la Typographie Néerlandaise au XVe Siècle. *La Haye*, 1874, 8vo

CAMUS (A. G.). Histoire et Procédés du Polytypage et de la Stéréotypie. *Paris, an X.* (1801) 8vo

CAMUS (A. G.). Mémoire sur les progrès, l'état actuel, et le perfectionnement de l'Imprimerie, &c. *Paris*, 1798, 4°

CAMUS (A. G.). Mémoire sur l'Impression des Cartes Géographiques, &c. *Paris*, 1798, 4°

CAMUS (A. G.). Notice d'un livre imprimé à Bamberg en 1462 par Albert Pfister. *Paris, an 7* (1799), 4°, *facsimiles, large paper*

CAPELLE (P.). Manuel de la Typographie Française ou traité complet de l'Imprimerie. Ouvrage utile aux jeunes typographes, aux libraires et aux gens de lettres. *Paris*, 1826, 4to

CAPIALBI (V.). Memorie delle tipografie Calabresi, con appendice sopra alcune biblioteche di Calabria, ed un discorso sulla tipografia Monteleonese. *Napoli*, 1835, 8°

CAPIALBI. Notizie circa la vita, le opere e le edizione di Messer Giovan Filippo da Legname Cavaliere Messinese e tipografo del secolo XV. *Napoli*, 1853, 8°

CAPITAINE (Ulysse). Bibliographie Liégeoise. 16e siècle. *Bruxelles*, 1852, 8° *Reprinted (200 copies) from the Bulletin du Bibliophile Belge, vol. ix.*

CAPITAINE (U.). Nouvelles Recherches sur les Impressions Liégeoises du XVIe Siècle. [*Bruxelles*, 1862], 8vo *Only 25 copies reprinted from the second series of the Bulletin, vol.* 2

CAPITAINE (U.). Nouvelles Recherches sur les Imprimeurs de Namur. *Bruxelles*, 1853, 8°

CARINI (F.). Istruzioni sopra l'arte tipografica per uso della gioventù Siciliana. *Palermo*, 1840, 4°

CARTON (C.). Colard Mansion et les Imprimeurs Brugeois du xve siècle. *Bruges*, 1848, 8°

CARUTTI (Domenico). Lorenzo Coster. Notizia intorno alla sua vita ed alla invenzione della Tipografia in Olanda. *Torino*, 1868, 4°

CASALI (Scipione). Annali della Tipografia Veneziana di Francesco Marcolini da Forlì. *Forlì*, 1861, 8°

CASLON. A specimen of Printing Types by W. Caslon and Son, Letter Founders, London, 1764, 8°

CASLON. A Specimen of large Letters by William Caslon. *London*, 1785, *a demy broadside*, f°

CASLON. Specimens of Printing Types by W. Caslon. *London*, 1796, 8*vo*

CASLON. Specimen of Printing Types by Henry Caslon, Chiswell Street, London, Letter Founder to Her Majesty's Honourable Board of Excise. *London*, 1841, 8°

CASLON. Specimen of Printing Types by Caslon and Livermore. *London*, 8*vo*

CASLON. Specimen of Printing Types of the Caslon and Glasgow Letter Foundry, 22, Chiswell Street, H. W. Caslon and Co. *London, impl.* 8°, a thick volume

CASTELEYN (Abraham), printer, of Haarlem. Reprint of the first number of " Weeckelycke Courante van Europa," 8 Jan. 1656, with a prospectus by Casteleyn. *Haarlem*, 1856, 4*to*

CATHERINOT (Nicolas). Annales Typographiques de Bourges. *Bourges*, 1683, 4°

CATHERINOT (N.). L'Art d'Imprimer. *Bourges*, 1685, 4°

CAVATTONI (Cesare). Due Memorie intorno l'antica Stampa Veronese. *Verona*, 1853, 8*vo*

CAXTON. The Game of the Chesse. [*Reprinted from Caxton's second edition by Vincent Figgins, with* 14 *pages of remarks on Typography of Caxton.*] *London*, 1855, 4*to*

CAXTON. The Statutes of Henry VII. in exact facsimile from the very rare original printed by Caxton in 1489, edited by John Rae. *London*, 1869, 4*to*

CAXTON. Life of William Caxton, with an account of the invention of Printing, and of the modes and materials used for transmitting knowledge before that took place. *London* [1832], 8*vo*

CAXTON and the Art of Printing. [*Religious Tract Society's Monthly Volume.*] *London*, 1850, 12mo

CAXTON. A Collection of Extracts, Cuttings, &c. relating to Caxton and early printing, made by Mr. Bolton Corney

CAZIN, sa Vie, et ses Editions, par un Cazinophile. *Cazinopolis* [Châlons], 1863, 12mo

CELLINI (Mariano). Note dei lavori della tipografia Galileiana e, per incidanza, Cenni sull' origine della Stampa e storia di detta tipografia. *Firenze*, 1862, 4º

CENNINI. Quarto Centenario Cenniniano. *Firenze*, 1871, 8º

CENNO di alcuni giureconsulti e chiari uomini di Chavasso; della prima Stamperia ivi aperta nel 1486, e di parecchie opere legali stampate in essa città. *Chivasso*, 1827, 8º

CHABERT. Histoire résumée de l'Imprimerie dans la Ville de Metz jusqu'au 19 siècle. *Metz*, 1851, 4º

CHABERT (L.). Stéréotypie et Polytypie. *Paris*, 1829, 4º

CHATTO (W. A.). Facts and Speculations on the Origin and History of Playing Cards. *London*, 1848, 8vo

CHATTO (W. A.). History and Art of Wood Engraving, ancient and modern, with Specimens selected from the "Illustrated London News," 1848; "The Bottle" and the Drunkard's Children, 16 plates by George Cruikshank, in 1 vol. *London*, 1848, *folio*

CHATTO (W. A.). A Treatise on Wood Engraving, historical and practical. With upwards of three hundred illustrations engraved on wood by J. Jackson. *London*, 1839, *imp.* 8vo

CHATTO (W. A.). A Treatise on Wood Engraving, historical and practical. *Inlaid on drawing cartridge paper, size 26 by 20 inches, extensively illustrated with many hundreds of engravings, woodcuts, etc., with specially printed title page and Preface, the whole bound in 3 vols.* 1839, *atlas folio*

These illustrations include many of the early woodcuts described in the Treatise, and the originals of others of which reduced facsimiles are therein given: Portraits of early Painters, Engravers, and Printers; a large number of old and scarce Chiaro-oscuros (the originals of those engraved in the work, and which therefore renders this collection more interesting and valuable), *old Title Pages, Initial Letters, and specimens of the various methods employed for the multiplication of copies by Printing, besides many fine impressions of Albert Durer's woodcuts and etchings (two of those etched on iron). The Chiaro-oscuros include specimens by Goltzius, Businck, De Trente, Le Sueur, Skippe, Kirkall, Jackson, and others. Among the woodcuts are fine impressions by Cranach, Urse Graf, Baldung, Jost Ammon, Christopher Jegher, as well as numerous examples of Bewick, Clennell, Nesbitt, and more modern artists*

CHATTO (W. A.). A Treatise on Wood Engraving, historical and practical, with upwards of three hundred illustrations engraved on wood by J. Jackson. The historical portion by W. A. Chatto. Second edition, with a new chapter on the artists of the present day, by H. G. Bohn, and 145 additional wood engravings. *London*, 1861, 8vo

CHATTO (W. A.). A Third Preface to " A Treatise on Wood Engraving, Historical and Practical," exposing the fallacies contained in the first, restoring the passages suppressed in the second, and containing an account of J. Jackson's actual share in the composition and illustration of that work. In a letter to Stephen Oliver. *London*, 1839, 8º

[CHELSUM (James).] A history of the Art of Engraving in Mezzotinto, from its origin to the present times, including an account of the works of the earliest artists. *Winchester*, 1786, 8vo

CHEVALLIER et LANGLUMÉ. Traité complet de Lithographie. *Paris*, 1838, 8º

CHEVILLIER (André). L'Origine de l'Imprimerie de Paris, dissertation, historique et critique, divisée en quatre parties. Dans la I. on voit son Etablissement qui fut fait par des Gens de l'Université, c'est-à-dire, par les soins de la Société de Sorbonne ; avec l'Histoire d'Ulric Gering, le premier Imprimeur de Paris. La II. contient des Reflexions sur les Livres imprimez par Gering, et quelques Remarques curieuses touchant les Imprimeurs, et sur la matière d'Imprimerie. La III. découvre l'origine de l'Impression Grecque et Hébraïque, qui fut établie à Paris par le soin des Professeurs de l'Université. Dans la IV. on fait voir les Droits que l'Université a eûs sur la Librairie de Paris, devant et après la découverte de l'Imprimerie. *Paris*, 1694, 4to

CICOGNARA (Leopold). Lettèra intorno ad alcune nuove scorperte e pratiche applicate all' arte dell' intaglio e dell' impressione. *No date*, 8*vo*

CICOGNARA (L.). Memorie spettanti alla storia della Calcografia. *Prato*, 1831, 8*vo*

CIRCOLARE della libreria Italiana. 2 vols. *Milano*, 1864-65, 8º (*All published*)

CIRIER (N.). L'œil typographique, offert aux hommes de lettres. *Paris*, 1839, 8*vo*

CLARENDON PRESS. A Specimen of the several sorts of Printing Types belonging to the University of Oxford at the Clarendon Printing House. 1786, 8*vo*

[CLARKE (Dr. Adam).] A Bibliographical Dictionary, containing a Chronological account, alphabetically arranged, of the most curious, scarce, useful, and important Books in all departments of literature, which have been published . . . from the infancy of Printing to the beginning of the nineteenth century. 6 vols. *Liverpool*, 1802-4, *small 8vo, large paper.* The Bibliographical Miscellany, or Supplement to the Bibliographical Dictionary. 2 vols. *London*, 1806, *small 8vo, large paper. The second volume contains a history of printing, list of authors on bibliography and typography, towns where printing was first carried on, &c.*

CLARKE (W.). Repertorium Bibliographicum; or, Account of celebrated British Libraries, with the Dialogue in the Shades and Rare Doings at Roxburghe Hall, a Poem, *with a variation of the Dialogue plate of which only 12 copies were struck off, and illustrated with additional portraits of Dr. Hunter, Earl Spencer, and Colonel Stanley.* London, 1819, 8*vo, large paper*

CLAYE (Jules). Manuel de l'Apprenti Compositeur, deuxième édition. *Paris*, 1874, 12*mo*

CLEEF (P. M. van). Alphabetisches naamlijst van fondsartikelen, waarvan het regt van eigendom aan anderen is overgegaan. *s'Grav.* 1839, 4*to. Interleaved, with numerous MS. additions*

[CLEEF (P. M. van)]. Handboek ter beoefening der boekdrukkunst in Nederland, voorafgegaan van eene beknopte geschiedenis dezer Kunst. *s'Gravenhage*, 1844, 8*vo*

CLÉMENT-JANIN. Recherches sur les imprimeurs

Dijonnais et sur les imprimeurs de la Côte-d'or. 1873, 8º

CLERGET (C. E.). De l'Ornementation Typographique [in French and German]. *Vienne*, 1859, 8vo

CLERICO (Giuseppe). Catalogo delle edizione di Tipografi di Trino nei Secoli XV. e XVI. *Torino*, 1870, 8vo

CLESSEN (Wilhelm Jeremias Jacob). Drittes Jubel-Fest der Buchdrucker-Kunst. Oder Christliches Denck- und Danckmahl dem allerhöchsten Gott zu Ehren, wegen der vor dreyhundert Jahren erfundenen und bisher erhaltenen edlen Buchdrucker-Kunst. Worinnen von Erfindung, Ausbreitung und Verbesserung, vom Nutzen, Lob und Fürtrefflichkeit, vom rechten Gebrauch und Misbrauch derselben gehandelt wird. *Gotha*, 1740, *small* 8vo

CLOWES. A description of Messrs. Clowes and Sons' Printing Office, Duke Street, Stamford Street, with a memoir of the late William Clowes, founder of the establishment. *London*, 8vo *For private circulation only. Reprinted from the " Quarterly Review" and " Days at the Factories"*

CLYMER (G.). Ueber die von G. Clymer in Philadelphia erfundene Patent-Columbia-Presse. *Braunschweig*, 1828, 4º

COCHET (l'Abbé J. B. D.). Histoire de l'Imprimerie à Dieppe. *Dieppe*, 1848, 8º

CODE de la Librairie et Imprimerie de Paris . . . . avec les anciens ordonnances . . . . au sujet de la Librairie et de l'Imprimerie depuis l'an 1332, jusqu'à présent. *Paris*, 1744, 12mo

COEN (Guiseppe). L'arte tipografica in Italia nell' ultimo decennio. *Firenze*, 1871, 16º

COLLECTION des lois relatives à l'imprimerie et à la librairie. *Amsterdam*, 1811, 8vo *In French and Dutch*

COLOGNE CHRONICLE (*containing a passage attributing the discovery of the Art of letterpress Printing to Guttenberg at Mayence*, 1440). Die Cronica van der hilliger Stat van Coellen. *Coellen*, 1499, *folio*

COLOMB DE BATINES (P. le Vicomte). Lettres à M. Jules Ollivier, contenant quelques documents sur l'origine de l'Imprimerie en Dauphiné. *Gap*, 1835, 8º

COLOMB DE BATINES. Matériaux pour servir à l'Histoire de l'Imprimerie en Dauphiné. *Gap,* 1837, 8º

COLOPHONS, Printers' Devices, Monograms, Title-pages, and Bibliographical Scraps. A collection alphabetically arranged

COLOSI (Giuseppe). Sul miglioramento della Stampa in Sicilia con quei mezzi che presenta: lettera. *Palermo,* 1857, 8º

COMI (Siro). Memorie bibliografiche per la Storia della Tipografia Pavese nel secolo XV. *Pavia,* 1807, 8º

CONFERENZA tra' signori prof. A. Migliorino e il bibliografo G. Mira sopra la stampa, se prima in Messina o contemporaneamente in Palermo sia stata introdotta. *Messina,* 1874, 8vo

CONFESSIONALE, ou Beichtspiegel nach den Zehn geboten, reproduit en facsimile d'après l'unique exemplaire conservé au Museum Meermanno-Westreenianum par E. Spanier. Avec une introduction par J. W. Holtrop. *La Haye,* 1861, *4to*

CONSTITUTION and By-laws of the Franklin Typographical Society of Cincinnati, &c. *Cincinnati,* 1849, 18º

CORRARD DE BREBAN. Les Graveurs Troyens. Recherches sur leur vie et leurs œuvres, avec facsimile. *Troyes,* 1868, 8vo *Only 170 copies printed*

CORRARD DE BREBAN. Recherches sur l'établissement et l'exercice de l'Imprimerie à Troyes, contenant la Nomenclature des Imprimeurs de cette Ville, depuis la fin du 15ᵉ Siècle jusqu'a 1789 et des Notices sur leurs productions les plus remarquables, avec facsimile. *Troyes,* 1839, *8vo*

CORRESPONDENT (der). Wochenschrift für Deutschlands Buchdrucker und Schriftgiesser, &c. *Leipzig,* 1863, 4º *In Progress*

COTTON (Henry). The Typographical Gazetteer. Second edition, corrected and much enlarged. *Oxford,* 1831, 8vo

COTTON (H.). A Typographical Gazetteer. Second Series. *Oxford,* 1866, 8º

COWELL (S. H.). A brief description of the Art of Anastatic Printing. *Ipswich,* 187–, *folio*

COWIE (GEORGE). Printers' Pocket Book and Manual, containing the compositors' and pressmen's scale of prices, &c. *London, n. d.* 12mo

Cowie (G.). Job-Master Printer's Price-Book. *London*, 1838, 8º

Crapelet (G. A.). De la Profession d'Imprimeur, des maîtres imprimeurs, &c. Liste générale des Imprimeurs de Paris depuis 1469 jusqu'en 1789. *Paris*, 1840, 8vo

Crapelet (G. A.). Des Brevets d'Imprimeur, des Certificats de capacité, &c. suivi du Tableau général des Imprimeries de toute la France en 1704, 1739, 1810, 1830 et 1840. *Paris*, 1840, 8vo

Crapelet (G. A.). Des Progrès de l'Imprimerie en France et en Italie au seizième siècle . . . . avec les Lettres Patentes de François Ier qui instituent le premier imprimeur royal pour le Grec. *Paris*, 1836, 8º

Crapelet (G. A.). Etudes Pratiques et Littéraires sur la Typographie. Tome premier (*all published*). *Paris*, 1837, 8vo

Crapelet (G. A.). Robert Estienne, Imprimeur Royal, et le Roi François Ier. Nouvelles recherches sur l'etat des lettres, et de l'Imprimerie au XVIe Siècle. *Paris*, 1839, 8vo

Cresswell (Rev. S. F.). Collections towards the History of Printing in Nottinghamshire, with an index of persons and subjects. *London*, 1863, small 4to

Crisp (William Finch). The Printer's Business Guide, &c. *London*, 1874, 8º

Crisp (W. F.). The Printer's Universal Book of Reference and Every-hour Office Companion. An Addendum to the Printer's Business Guide. *London*, 1875, 8º

Cumberland (George). Hints to various modes of Printing from autographs. [*Nicholson's Journal*, vol. xxxviii. p. 56.] 1811, 8º

D —— (R——). Laurenz Janz Koster: Jaarboekje voor Typographische Vereenigingen. *Leyden*, 1856, 12º

DAHL (J. C.). Die Buchdruckerkunst erfunden von Johann Gutenberg verbessert und zur Vollkommenheit gebracht durch Peter Schöffer von Gernsheim: Historisch-kritische Abhandlung. *Mainz*, 1832, 8*vo*

DAHL (J. C.). Peter Schöffer von Gernsheim, Miterfinder der Buchdruckerkunst. Eine historische Skizze, mit einer kurzen Geschichte der Erfindung jener Schönen Kunst überhaupt. *Wiesbaden*, 1814, 8*vo*

DANNA (Casimiro). Dell' arte tipografica festeggiata in Saluzzo e Mondovì nell' Ottobre del 1872. Memorie e discorso. *Mondovi*, 1872, 8º

DAUNOU (P. C. F.). Analyse des Opinions diverses sur l'Origine de l'Imprimerie. *Paris*, an xi. [1803], 8*vo*

DAVENPORT (S. T.). Engraving and other reproductive Art Processes. *In the " Journal of the Society of Arts,"* Jan. 13, 1865. *London*, 8º

DAVIES (Robert). A memoir of the York Press, with notices of authors, printers, and stationers in the sixteenth, seventeenth, and eighteenth centuries. *Westminster*, 1868, 8*vo*

DEARBORN (N.). American Text Book of Letters. *Boston*, 1846, 4*to*

DECLARATION du Roy, Donnée à Fontainebleau le 2 d'Octobre, 1701. Portant Reglement pour les Libraires et Imprimeurs. *Grenoble*, 1701, 4*to*

DELALAIN (Jules). Legislation de l'Imprimerie d'après la nouvelle Loi de la Presse. Suivie d'un tableau des cas de responsabilité et de pénalité auxquels sont soumis les Imprimeurs. *Paris*, 1868, 12º

DELALAIN (J.). Recueil de Documents Officiels relatifs au Régime de l'Imprimerie. *Paris*, 1867, 8º

DELALAIN (J.). La Typographie Française et Etrangère à l'Exposition Universelle. *Paris*, 1855, 8*vo*

DE LA MOTTE (P. H.). On the various applications of Anastatic Printing and Papyrography. With illustrative examples. *London*, 1849, 8*vo*

DELANDINE (F. A.). Histoire abrégée de l'Imprimerie, ou précis sur son origine, son établissement en France, etc. 1814, 8º

DELESCHAMPS (Pierre). Des Mordants, des vernis et des planches dans l'art du graveur, ou Traité complet de la Gravure. *Paris*, 1836, 8º

DELPRAT (G. H. M.). Dissertation sur l'Art Typographique contenant un aperçu historique de ses progrès durant le XV. et le XVI. siècle et des recherches sur l'influence de cet art sur les lumières de l'espèce humaine. *Utrecht*, 1820, 8*vo*

DEMBOUR (A.). Description d'un nouveau procédé de gravure en relief sur cuivre. *Metz*, 1835, 4º

DEMBOUR (A.). Die Metall-Ektypographie, &c. *Braunschweig*, 1835, 4º

DENIS (Michael). Bibliotheca Typographica Vindobonensis, ab anno 1482 ad annum 1560. *Vindobonæ*, 1782, 4*to*

DENIS (M.). Suffragium pro Johanne de Spirâ, primo Venetiarum typographo. *Viennæ*, 1794, 8*vo*

DENIS (M.). Wiens Buchdruckergeschichte bis 1560. *Wien*, 1782, 4*to*

DENIS (M.). Nachtrag zu seiner Buchdruckergeschichte Wiens. *Wien*, 1793, 4º

DESBARREAUX-BERNARD (T.). La Chasse aux Incunables. *Toulouse*, 1864, 8*vo* *Only one hundred copies printed*

DESBARREAUX-BERNARD (T.). L'Imprimerie à Toulouse aux XVe.—XVIIe. siècles. *Toulouse*, 1865, 8º

DESBARREAUX-BERNARD (T.). Quelques recherches sur les débuts de l'Imprimerie à Toulouse. *No date*. 8*vo*

DESPORTES (M. J.). Manuel pratique du Lithographe. *Paris*, 1834, 8º

DESPREAUX. Note detaillée sur l'invention de la gravure en relief. *Paris*, 1836, 4º

DESROCHES (J.). Nieuw Onderzoek naar den Oorsprong der Boekdrukkunst. *Amsterdam*, 1778, 8º

DESROCHES (J.). Nouvelles recherches sur l'origine de l'Imprimerie, dans lesquelles on fait voir que la première idée en est due aux Brabançons. *In vol. 1 of the Collections de l'Académie de Bruxelles. Bruxelles*, 1777, 4to

DESTANBERG (N.). Laurens Coster. Drama in dry bedryven. *Antwerpen*, 1855, 8º

DEUTSCHE PRESSE (die). Wochen-journal. *Aschersleben*, 1862, fº *In Progress*

DE VINNE (Theodore L.). The Invention of Printing. A Collection of Facts and Opinions descriptive of Early Prints and Playing Cards, the Block Books of the fifteenth century, the Legend of Lourens Janszoon Coster of Haarlem, and the work of John Gutenberg and his associates. Illustrated with Facsimiles of Early Types and Woodcuts. *New York*, 1876, 8vo

DE VINNE (T. L.). The Printer's Price List. A Manual for the use of Clerks and Book-keepers in Job Printing Offices. *New York*, 1871, 12mo

DE VINNE (T. L.). The State of the Trade. Observations on Eight Hours and High Prices, suggested by recent conferences between the New York Typographical Union and the Employing Book and Job printers of that City. *New York*, 1872, 8vo

DIBDIN (Rev. Thomas Frognall). The Bibliographical Decameron, or ten days pleasant discourse upon illuminated manuscripts and subjects connected with early Engraving, Typography, and Bibliography. 3 vols. *London*, 1817, 8vo. [*The author's copy*]

DIBDIN (T. F.). Bibliomania; or Book-madness, a Bibliographical Romance. Illustrated with cuts. New and improved edition, to which are now added Preliminary Observations, and a Supplement, including a Key to the assumed characters in the Drama. *London*, 1842, *royal 8vo*

DIBDIN (T. F.). Lettre trentième concernant l'imprimerie et la librairie de Paris, traduite avec des notes par G. A. Crapelet. *Paris*, 1821, 4to

DICKINSON (Samuel N.). A Help to Printers and Publishers; being a Series of Calculations, showing the quantity of Paper required for a given number of Signatures in book work, and the number of Tokens contained therein; carried out to an extent that will seldom, if ever, fail to embrace the largest jobs. Also a table for Job Work, showing the quantity of Paper required for a given number of bills, labels, duplicates of book work, &c. *Boston*, 1835, 8vo

DICKINSON (S. N.). Specimen of Book Printing. *Boston*, 1842, *royal 8vo*

DIDOT (Ambroise Firmin). Alde Manuce et l'Hellénisme a Venise. *Paris*, 1875, 8vo

DIDOT (A. F.). Les Alde Manuce. *Paris*, 1860, 8vo [*Extract from Nouvelle Biographie Générale*]

DIDOT (A. F.). Essai sur la Typographie. *Paris*, 1851, 8vo, *plates*

DIDOT (A. F.). Essai Typographique et Bibliographique sur l'histoire de la Gravure sur Bois. *Paris*, 1863, 8vo

DIDOT (A. F.). Les Drevet (Pierre, Pierre-Imbert et Claude). Catalogue Raisonné de leur œuvre précédé d'une introduction. *Paris*, 1876, 8vo

DIDOT (A. F.). Les Estienne. Henri I.; François I. et II.; Robert I. II. et III.; Henri II.; Paul et Antoine. Extrait de la Nouvelle Biographie Générale. [*Paris*, 1865], 8º

DIDOT (A. F.). L'Imprimerie, la Librairie et la Papeterie à l'Exposition Universelle de 1851. *Paris*, 1854, 8vo *Fine paper*

DIDOT. Vecellio (Cesare) Costumes Anciens et Modernes. Habiti Antichi e Moderni di tutto il Mondo. Précédés d'un Essai sur la Gravure sur bois. 2 vols. *Paris*, 1860, 8vo

DIDOT (Pierre). Epitre sur les progrès de l'Imprimerie. *Paris*, 1784, *royal 8º*

DIDOT (P.). Lettre sur les Découvertes de M. Didot, l'aîné, dans les Arts de l'Imprimerie, de la Gravure des Caractères, et de la Papeterie. [*Paris*, 1783], 8º

DIDOT (P.). Specimen des nouveaux Caractères. *Paris*, 1819, 8vo

DINGLESTEDT (Franz). Jean Gutenberg, premier maître imprimeur, ses faits et discours les plus dignes d'admiration, et sa mort. Traduit de l'allemand par Gustave Revilliod. *Genève*, 1858, *small folio*. *6 etchings by Gandon on India paper. Only a small number printed*

DINGELSTEDT (F.). John Gutenberg, first master printer, his acts and most remarkable discourses, and his Death. From the German by C[aroline] W[intour]. *London*, 1860, 8vo *100 copies printed*

DINGELSTEDT (F.). Sechs Jahrhundert aus Gutenberg's Leben. Kleine Gabe zum grossen Feste. *Cassel*, 1840, folio. *Woodcuts, with explanations by F. Muller*

DOCUMENTS Iconographiques et Typographiques de la Bibliothèque Royale de la Belgique. Livr. 1—4. *Bruxelles*, 1864-71, folio. *Photolithographic plates. All yet published*

DODT VAN FLENSBURG (J. J.). Over de Elzevier's. *Utrecht*, 1841, 8vo

DOEDES (J. I.). Lourens Janszoon Coster, Johan Guttenberg en Peter Schöffer. *Review of works by Vries and Noordziek, re-printed from the Gids, No. 12.* [*Amsterdam*, 1849], 8vo

DORLAN (A.). Quelques Mots sur l'origine de l'Imprimerie, ou Résumé des opinions qui en attribuent l'invention à Jean Mentel, natif de Schlestadt. *Schlestadt*, 1840, 8vo *Portrait and 6 plates of facsimile*

DRAUDIUS (George). Discursus Typographicus, cum Præcipiorum Typographorum insignibus, eorundemque expositionibus conjecturalibus. *Francof.* 1625, 8º

DUCHESNE (Jean). Essai sur les Nielles, Gravures des Orfèvres Florentins du XVᵉ Siècle. *Paris*, 1826, 4to

DUNST (J. M.). Praektisches Lehrbuch der Lithographie und Steindruckerkunst. *Bonn*, 1836, 8º

DUPLESSIS (Georges). De la Gravure de Portrait en France. *Paris*, 1875, 8vo

DUPLESSIS (G.). Essai de bibliographie, contenant l'indication des ouvrages relatifs à l'histoire de la Gravure et des Graveurs. *Paris*, 1862, 8vo

DUPLESSIS (G.). Histoire de la Gravure en France. *Paris*, 1861, 8vo

DUPLESSIS (G.). Les Merveilles de la Gravure. Ouvrage illustré par P. Sellier. *Paris*, 1869, 8vo

DUPLESSIS (G.). The Wonders of Engraving. Illustrated with ten reproductions in Autotype, and thirty-four wood engravings by P. Sellier. *London*, 1871, 8vo

DUPLESSIS (G.). Notice sur la vie et les travaux de Gérard Audran, graveur ordinaire du Roi. *Paris*, 8º *Only 100 copies printed*

DUPONT (Paul). 1851. Exposition Universelle de Londres. Notice concernant l'établissement Typographique de M. Paul Dupont de Paris. *Paris, 1851*, 8º *In French and English*

DUPONT (P.). Histoire de l'Imprimerie. 2 vols. *Paris, 1854, 8vo, large paper in impl. 8vo*

DUPONT (P.). Mémoire sur la Litho-typographie, &c. *Paris, 1839, 4º, 8 pages of specimens*

DUPONT (P.). Notice Historique sur l'Imprimerie. *Paris, 1849, 4º*

DUPONT (P.). Une Imprimerie en 1867. *Paris, 1867, impl. 8vo*

DUPRAT (F. A.). Aperçu sur la progrès de la Typographie depuis le XVIᵉ siècle et sur l'état actuel de l'Imprimerie de Paris. *Paris, 1863, 8vo Extract from the Bulletin du Bouquiniste. Only 100 copies printed*

DUPRAT (F. A.). Histoire de l'Imprimerie Impériale de France, suivie des specimens des Types Étrangers et Français de cet établissement. *Paris, 1861, 8vo*

DUPRAT (F. A.). Précis Historique sur l'Imprimerie Nationale et ses Types. *Paris, 1848, 8vo*

DUSSEAU (P. I. V.). De Boekdrukkunst en derzelver uitvinder Laurens Jansz. Koster. *Amsterdam* [1839], 12º

BERT (Prof. F. A.). Nieuw Ondezoek naar de Aanspraak van Holland op de uitvinding der Boekdrukkunst; en brief wegens het Geschrift van Prof. F. Lehne met een vorrede en eenige aanmerkingen van J. Koning. *Haarlem, 1825, 8vo*

ECKSTEIN (F. A.). Die Sahlfeldschen Buchdruckereien in Halle. *Halle, 1842, 4to*

ED (C. M.). Kurzgefasste Geschichte der Buchdruckerkunst. *Hamburg, 1840, 12mo*

ED (C. M.). Kurzgefasste Geschichte des Buchdrucks. *Hamburg, 1839, 8vo*

EDEL (Friedrich Wilhelm). Denkschrift für die im Jahr 1840 zu begenhende vierte Säcularfeier der Erfindung der Buchdruckerkunst. *Strassburg, 1840, 12mo*

EDWARDS & KIDD, Printers, London. International Exhibition, 1871. The Heliotype Process. *London, 1871, 8º*

EEKHOFF (W.). Nieuwe Bijdrage tot de Geschiedenis van de Boekdrukkunst in Nederland; bevattende een betoog, dat de eerst druk van de Oude Friesche Wetten, bezorgd door Heer H. Cammingha omstreeks 1484 is gedrukt te Leeuwarden. *Workum, 1856, 8vo*

EICHSFELD (E. G.). Relation vom Wittebergischen Buchdrucker-Jubiläo, 1740. Nebst eine historische Nachricht von allen Wittenbergischen Buchdruckern. *Wittenberg, 1740, 4º*

EISENMANN (A.). Die Schnellpresse, ihre Construction, Zusammen-Stellung und Behandlung. *Leipzig, 1865, 4º*

EKAMA (Dr. C.). Romeyn de Hooghe en de Hortus Medicus met het standbeeld van L. J. Coster. *Haarlem, 1869, 8vo*

ELECTROTYPER, The, Quarterly. *Chicago, 1873, 4to*
In Progress

ELLIS (Henry). Copies of Original Papers illustrative of the management of Literature by Printers and Stationers in the middle of the reign of Queen Elizabeth. Article in the *Archæologia*, vol. xxv., pp. 100-112. *London, 1834, 4º*

ELVERT (Christian d'). Geschichte des Bücher-und Steindruckes, des Buchhandels, der Bücher-Censur, und der periodischen Literatur, so wie Nachträge zur Geschichte der historichen Literatur in Mähren und Oesterreichisch-Schlesien. *Brünn, 1854, 8vo*

ELZEVIR. Catalogus librorum officinæ Dan. Elsevirii. *Amst. 1681, 12mo Re-impression by Didot, edited by Ch. Motteley. Paris, 1823, 12mo*
One hundred copies printed

ELZEVIR. Over het aantal Drukkers, uit de familie der Elzeviers voortgesproten. [*Algemeene Konsten Letter-Bode*, No. 8.] *1807, 8vo*

ELZEVIR. A collection of MS. Notes by Mr. Bodel Nyenhuis, &c., relating to the Elzevir family

EMERIC-DAVID (Toussaint Bernard). Discours historique sur la Gravure en taille-douce et sur la Gravure en bois. *Paris*, 1808, 8º

EMERIC-DAVID (T. B.). Histoire de la Peinture au Moyen Age, suivie de l'Histoire de la Gravure, &c. *Paris*, 1863, 12º

ENGEL (S.). Lettre sur l'Origine de l'Imprimerie et sur diverses éditions anciennes. *Berne*, 1742, 8º

ENGELHARD-REYHERSCHEN. Schrift-Proben aus der Buchdruckerey in Gotha. [1826], 8*vo*

ENGELMANN (G.). Das Gesammtgebiet der Lithographie, oder theoretische und praktische Anleitung zur Ausübung der Lithographie in ihrem ganzen Umfange. Uebertragung des "Traité Théorique et Pratique de Lithographie," mit den nöthigen zusätzen versehen von W. Pabst und A. Kretzschman. *Leipzig*, 1847, 4º

ENGELMANN (G.). Traité théorique et pratique de la Lithographie. *Mulhouse*, 1838, 4to 50 *plates*

ENQUIRY (An), into the origin of Printing in Europe by a Lover of the Art. *London*, 1752, 8º

ENSCHEDÉ (Isaac et Jean). Epreuve de Caractères qui se fondent dans la nouvelle Fonderie. 1748, 8*vo*

ENSCHEDÉ (Joannes). Proef van Letteren, uit de Lettergietery van. *Haarlem*, 1768, 8*vo*

ENSCHEDÉ (J.). Proef van Letteren, welke gegooten worden in de nieuwe Haerlemsche Lettergietery. [*Haerlem*], 1768, 8*vo*

ENSCHEDÉ. Berigt en Proeve van de nieuwe Javaansche drukletters, naar het voorschrift en onder toezigt van T. Roorda, vervaardigt ter lettergieterij van Joh. Enschedé en zonen te Haarlem. 4º

ENSCHEDÉ. Epreuves d'une première Imprimerie Javanaise, dont les Caractères ont été confectionnés, d'après le projet et sous la direction de P. van Vlissingen à la fonderie de Jean Enschedé et fils à Harlem. *Harlem*, 1824, 4º

ENSCHEDÉ EN ZOONEN. Proeve van Letteren, &c. *Haarlem*, 1806, 8*vo*

ENSCHEDÉ ET FILS. Specimen de Caractères Typographiques anciens qui se trouvent dans la

Collection Typographique de J. Enschedé et fils, imprimeurs à Harlem. *Haarlem*, 1869, 4to *One hundred copies printed*

ERASMUS. Erasmi Roteradami Silva Carminum antehac nunquam impressorum Gouda, 1513. Reproduction photo-lithographique avec notice par M. Ch. Ruelens. *Bruxelles*, 1864, 4to *Only one hundred copies printed*

ERICHSON (Johann). Die Heilsahmen Absichten, welche Gott bey Erfindung und zeitiger Einführung der Edlen Buchdrucker-Kunst in hiesige Reiche. Besonders zu dieser Ihrem Besten, gehabt. In einer kurtzen Rede, welche den 10. Nov. dieses 1740 sten Jahres dieser herrlichen Kunst. In der Teutschen Schule hieselbst öffentlich gehalten worden. *Stockholm* [1740], 4to

ERNESTI (J. H. G.). Die wohleingerichtete Buchdruckerey, mit 120 Teutsch-Lateinisch-Griechisch und Hebräischen Schrifften . . . . nebst einer summarischen Nachricht von der Buchdruckern in Nürnberg, &c. *Nürnberg*, 1733, *oblong* 4to

ERSCH (J. S.) und GRUBER (J. G.). Allgemeine Encyclopädie der Wissenschaften und Künste, vol. 14. *Leipzig*, 1825, 4to [*Containing long article on Printing by Poppe, Ebert and Dahl*]

ESCHER (H.). Kommentar zu dem im Kanton Zürich geltenden Gesetz, betreffend die Druckerpresse. *Zurich*, 1829, 8º

ESCODECA DE BOISSE. Exposition Universelle de 1855. Quelques détails sur les Produits de l'Imprimerie Impériale de France. *Paris*, 1855, 8vo

ESSAY on the Original, Use, and Excellency of the Noble Art and Mystery of Printing. *London*, 1752, 8º

ESSENWEIN (A.). Aelteste Druckerzeugnisse im Germanischen Museum. *Illustrated articles in "Anzeiger fur künde der Deutschen Vorzeit," Nos. 8 and 9.* Nürnberg, 1872, 4to

EVELYN (John). Sculptura: or the history and art of Chalcography and Engraving in Copper. *London*, 1769, *small* 8vo

EVEN (Edward van). De Elzeviers te Leuven in de 16ᵉ eeuw. 1850, 8º

EVEN (E. van). Notice sur Pierre Werrecoren, Imprimeur à St. Maertensdyk, en Zélande (1478).

Bruxelles, 1851, 8vo   Reprinted from the Bulletin du Bibliophile Belge, vol. 8

EVEN (E. van). Renseignements inédits sur les imprimeurs de Louvain, au 15ᵉ siècle. [Bruxelles, 1865], 8vo   Reprinted from the Bibliophile Belge

EVEN (E. van). Rudolf Loeffs, drukker te Bommel, 1491. (Utrecht, 1853), 8º

EVERY Man his own Printer, or Lithography made Easy: being an Essay upon Lithography in all its branches, showing more particularly the advantages of the Patent Autographic Press. London, 1854, royal 8vo   Portrait of Senefelder and 9 plates

EXHIBITION OF 1851. Catalogue, vol. ii. sect. iii. class 17. Paper and Stationery, Printing and Bookbinding—also Reports of the Juries. Royal 8vo   The Report on Printing is signed by A. Firmin Didot, C. Whittingham, and T. De la Rue

EYRE AND SPOTTISWOODE. Her Majesty's Printing Office. A general Specimen of Printing Types, &c., &c. London, 1861, 8º

FABRICIUS (J. F.). Notizen über die Einführung und erste Ausbreitung der Buchdruckerkunst in Amerika. Hamburg, 1841, small 8º

FACCIO (Domenico). Notizie storico-tipografiche di Guttemberg, Fust e Schöffer, primi inventori della stampa. Padova, 1846, 8º

FACCIOLI (Tomasso). Catalogo ragionato dei libri stampati in Vicenza e suo territorio nel secolo XV. con un' Appendice de' libri de' Vicentini o spettanti a Vicenza che in quel secolo si stamparono altrove. Vicenza, 1796, 8vo

FAIN (A.). Epreuves de Caractères de la Fonderie et de l'Imprimerie de A. Fain. Paris, 1832, 8vo

FAITHORNE (William). The Art of graveing and etching, wherein is exprest the true way of graveing in Copper. Also the manner and method of Callot and Mr. Bosse in their severall ways of etching. London, 1702, 12mo

FALKENSTEIN (C. von). Geschichte der Buchdruckerkunst in ihrer Entstehung und Ausbildung. Ein Denkmal zur vierten Säcular-Feier der Erfindung der Typographie. Mit einer reichen Sammlung in Holz und Metall geschnittener Facsimiles der seltensten Holtztafeldrucke. Nachbildungen von Typen alter berühmter officinen und Proben von Kunstdrucken nach den neuesten Erfindungen unserer Zeit. *Leipzig*, 1840, 4to *Numerous facsimile plates, and at end 10 leaves of specimens of Oriental type*—2nd edition, *Leipzig*, 1856, 4º

FANTOZZI (Federigo). **Notizie** biografiche originali di Bernardo Cennini, **orafo** Fiorentino, primo promotore della tipografia in Firenze, con indicazione della casa e della botteghe ove abitò ed esercitò l'arte. *Firenze*, 1839, 8º

FAULMANN (Karl). **Neue** Untersuchungen über die entstehung der Buchstabenschrift und die Person des Erfinders. *Wien*, 1876, 8vo

[FEDERICI (Domenico Maria).] Memorie **Tre**vigiane sulla Tipografia del secolo XV. per servire alla Storia Litteraria e delle Belle **Arti** d'Italia. *Venezia*, 1805, 4to

FEDERICI (**F.**). Annali **della** Tipografia Volpi-Cominiana **colle** Notizie **intorno** la Vita e gli Studj de fratelli Volpi. *Padova*, 1809, 8vo *Portrait of G. A. Volpi and one plate.* Appendice agli Annali della Tipografia Volpi-Cominiana. *Padova*, 1817, 8vo

FEENY (**R.**). Master-Printer's Price-Manual, to which **is** added Specimens **of** Type in general use; with the proper manner **of** marking corrections in **a** proof-sheet; also a list of wholesale Stationers. *London*, **1845, 12º**

FELDER (R. M.). **Des** Buchdruckers Erdenleben mit seinen Licht-und Schattenseiten. Ein schöner Traum und das Erwachen. *Stuttgart*, 1839, **16mo**

FERGUSON BROTHERS. Specimen of the Aldine series of new Founts. *Edinburgh, oblong fº*

FERGUSON BROTHERS. Specimens of new Book and Newspaper Founts. *Edinburgh, oblong fº*

FERGUSON BROTHERS. Specimens of Wood **Letter**. *Edinburgh, oblong 4º 56 leaves*

FERRARIO. Le classiche stampe dal Cominciamento della Calcografia fino al presente. *Milano*, 1836, 8vo

FERTEL (Martin Dominique). La Science Pratique de l'Imprimerie, Contenant des **Instructions** très faciles pour se perfectionner dans cet art. On y trouvera une description de toutes les pièces dont une presse est construite, avec une methode pour imposer toutes sortes d'impositions. *St. Omer*, 1723, 4*to*

FESTIVALS. Books of words of songs, programmes, and pamphlets relating to the several festivals commemorative of the discovery of Printing, with many MS. notes of Mr. Bodel Nuyenhuis—an interesting and large collection

FEST-TAGE des Buchdruckers, Die. Eine Sammlung von Prologen, Festgrüssen, Tafelliedern, Gedichten zu Jubiläen, Toasten, etc. *Leipzig*, 1868, 12*mo*

FICKENSCHER (G. W. A.). Geschichte der Buchdruckerwesens im Burggrafthum Nürnberg, &c. *Bayreuth*, 1802, 8°

FIELDING (Theodore H.). The Art of Engraving, with the various modes of operation. Illustrated with specimens of the different styles of engraving. *London*, 1841, royal 8°

FIGGINS (V.). Specimen of Printing Types, etc. *London*, 1821, 8*vo*

FIGGINS (V. and J.). Specimens of Book and Newspaper Types. *London*, 1838, 4*to*

FIGGINS (V. and J.). Specimen of Printing Types by V. & J. Figgins, successors to Vincent Figgins, Letter Founder. *London*, 1838, 8*vo*

FIGGINS (V. and J.). Specimen of Printing Types. *London*, 1842, royal 8*vo*

FILS (G.). Art de l'Imprimerie-Librairie, composé en 1795, quant au mécanisme typographique. *Paris*, 1836, 4°

FINESCHI (Vincenzio). Notizie Storiche sopra la Stamperia di Ripoli, lequali possono servire all' illustrazione della Storia Tipografica Fiorentina. *Firenze*, 1781, 8*vo*

FISCHER (Gotthelf). Beschreibung einiger typographischen Seltenheiten, nebst Beyträgen zur Erfindungs Geschichte der Buchdruckerkunst. *Mainz und Nürnberg*, 1800-1804, 8*vo*, *numerous facsimiles*

FISCHER (G.). Essai sur les Monumens Typographiques de Jean Gutenberg Mayençais, inventeur de l'Imprimerie. *Mayence*, [1802], 4*to*

FISCHER (G.). Geschichte der seit dreyhundert Jahren in Breslau befindlichen Stadtbuchdruckerei. *Breslau*, 1804, 4º

FISCHER (G.). Notice du Premier Monument Typographique, en caractères Mobiles, avec date, connu jusqu'à ce jour. *Mayence*, 1804, 4to

FLATHE (Ludwig). Die vierte Säcular-Feier der erfindung Gutenbergs in Dresden und Leipzig. Ein Gedenkbuch für Gegenwart und Zukunft. *Leipzig*, 1840, 8vo

FLICK (J. F.). Beschreibung der elastischen Auftragewalzen in den Buchdruckereien, deren Anfertigung, etc. *Leipzig*, 1823, 8º

FLICK (J. F.). Handbuch der Buchdruckerkunst, für angehende und praktische Buckdrucker. Als anhang anweisung, Papiere auf alle Art zu färben. Mit einem Vollständigen Formatbuche der Vorstellung einer Correctur und vier Kastenabbildungen in Steindruck. *Berlin*, 1820, 8º

FLICK (J. F.). Kleines Hand-und Hülfsbuch für Buchhändler, Schriftsteller und Correktoren, mit der Vorstellung einer Correktur. Vom Verfasser des Handbuchs für Buckdrucker. *Rathenow*, 1821, 8º

FOLDS (George). Specimens of Irish Typography: illustrative of the National Press of Ireland. *Dublin*, 1833, 8vo

FONCEMAGNE (Etienne Lauréault de). Examen de M. Maittaire touchant l'époque de l'établissement de l'Imprimerie en France. In vol. vii. *of Mémoires de l'Académie des Inscriptions et Belles Lettres*. *Paris*, 1743, 4º

FORD (J.). **Compositor's Hand-Book.** *London*, 1854, 12º

FORMAT-BUCHLEIN, ou Tableau de tous les Formats d'Imprimerie depuis l'in-folio jusqu'à l'in-128. [*no place*], 1673, oblong 4º

FORMS. Het overslaan van Drukvormen gemakkelijk gemaakt. *Deventer*, 1843, 12mo

FORTIER (G.). La Photolithographie, son Origine, ses Procédés, ses Applications. *Paris*, 1876, 8vo

FOUDRIAT ET PENNEQUIN. Epreuve des Caractères. *Bruxelles*, 1828, 4to

FOUGT (H.). Specimens of a new Type for Music; in six sonatas by Uttini. 3 vols. *London*, 1768, fº

Fournier (Henri). Essai sur l'Imprimerie par un jeune ouvrier imprimeur. *Bordeaux*, 1802, 8º

Fournier (H.). Traité de la Typographie. *Paris*, 1825, 8vo—Deuxième édition, corrigée et augmentée. *Paris*, 1854, small 8vo

Fournier (Pierre Simon). Les Caractères de l'Imprimerie. *Paris*, 1764, *small* 8vo

Fournier (P. S.). Dissertation sur l'Origine et les Progrès de l'Art de graver en bois, pour éclaircir quelques traits de l'histoire de l'imprimerie, et prouver que Guttemberg n'en est pas l'Inventeur. *Paris*, 1758, 8vo

Fournier (P. S.). Lettre a M. Fréron au sujet de l'édition d'une Bible annoncée pour être la première production de l'Imprimerie. *Paris*, 1763, 8º

Fournier (P. S.). Lettre sur l'origine de l'Imprimerie, servant de réponse aux "Observations" publié par Fournier le Jeune, sur l'ouvrage de Schœpflin intitulé : Vindiciæ typographicæ. *Strasbourg*, 1761, 8º

Fournier (P. S.). Manuel typographique, utile aux gens de lettres et à ceux qui exercent les différentes parties de l'art de l'imprimerie. 2 vols. *Paris*, 1764-66, 8vo

Fournier (P. S.). Observations sur un ouvrage intitulé: Vindiciæ Typographicæ. *Paris*, 1760, 8vo

Fournier (P. S.). De l'Origine et des Productions de l'Imprimerie primitive en taille de bois, avec une réfutation des prejugés plus ou moins accrédités sur cet Art; pour servir de suite à la Dissertation sur l'origine de l'Art de graver en bois. *Paris*, 1759, 8vo

Fournier (P. S.). Remarques sur un ouvrage intitulé : Lettres sur l'Origine de l'Imprimerie, pour servir de suite au traité, " De l'origine et des productions de l'Imprimerie primitive en taille de bois." *Paris*, 1761, 8º

Fournier (P. S.). Table des Proportions des Caractères d'Imprimerie. *Paris*, 1737, 4º

Fournier (P. S.). Traité Historique et Critique sur l'Origine et les Progrès des Caractères de Fonte, pour l'Impression de la Musique, avec des Epreuves de nouveaux Caractères de Musique. *Berne*, 1765, 4º

France. Notice sur les Types étrangers du Spécimen de l'Imprimerie Royale. *Paris, f*º

Francis (Jabez). **Printing at Home, with full instructions for Amateurs**: containing illustrations of the necessary materials, with explanatory key, specimens of type, etc. *Rochford, Essex,* [1869], *small 8vo With 8 leaves of Specimens, etc.*

Franke (C. A.). Handbuch der Buchdruckerkunst. *Weimar,* 1867, *cr. 8vo*

Franke (C. A.). Katechismus der Buchdruckerkunst. *Leipzig,* 1856, *12mo*

Franklin (Alfred). La Sorbonne, ses origines, sa bibliothèque, les débuts de l'imprimerie à Paris, et la succession de Richelieu, d'après des documents inédits; **2e** édition. *Paris,* 1875, *8vo*

Franklin (Benjamin). Autobiography; **with a** Narrative of his Public Life and Services by H. Hastings Weld. *New York,* 1848, *8vo*

Franklin Statue. Record of the Proceedings and Ceremonies pertaining to the Erection of the Franklin Statue in Printing House Square, presented by Albert de Groot to the Press and Printers of the City of New York. *New York,* 1872, *8vo*

Freissauf von Neudegg (F.). Beschreibung der Ektypograph für Alinde, &c. *Wien,* 1837, 4º

Frère (Edouard). Considérations sur les origines Typographiques. *Rouen,* 1850, 8º *Extract from Précis des Travaux de l'Académie de Rouen*

Frère (E.). De l'Imprimerie et de la Librairie à Rouen, dans les xve et xvie siècles, et de Martin Morin, célèbre imprimeur rouennais. *Rouen,* 1843, *8vo*

Frère (E.). Des Livres de liturgie des Eglises d'Angleterre (Salisbury, York, Hereford) imprimés à Rouen dans les xve et xvie siècles. Etude suivie du Catalogue de ces impressions de mccccxcii à mdlvii, avec des notes bibliographiques. *Rouen,* 1867, 8º *Only* **125** *copies printed*

Frère (E.). Manuel du Bibliographe Normand ou dictionnaire historique et bibliographique des recherches sur l'Histoire de l'Imprimerie en Normandie. 2 vols. *Rouen,* 1858, *royal 8vo*

Frère (E.). Recherches sur les premiers temps de l'Imprimerie en Normandie. *Rouen,* 1829, 8º

Frese (J. H.). Die doppelte Buch-und Geschäftsführung für Buchdruckereien und verwandte Geschäfte. *Leipzig,* 1869, *4to*

FRESENIUS (J. F. Th.). Zur Geschichte der Erfindung des Buchdrucks. Einladungschrift zu den auf den 28sten, 29sten, und 30sten April und den 1sten Mai 1840 festgesetzten öffentlichen Prüfungen in der Mittelschule. *Frankfurt am Main*, 1840, *8vo*

(FREY A.). Manuel Nouveau de Typographie imprimerie, contenant les principes théoriques et pratiques de l'imprimeur typographe. Ouvrage original. 2 vols. *Paris*, 1835, *18mo*

FREY (A.). Nouveau Manuel Complet de Typographie. 2 vols. *Paris*, 1857, *12mo*

FREYBERG (C. A.). Reliquien von der Dressdnischen und übrigen Ober-Sachsischen Buchdrucker-Historie. *Dressden*, 1741, *4to*

FREYBERG (C. A.). Von der allerersten und ältesten Buchdruckern zu Dressden. *Dressden*, 1740, *4to*

FREYLINGHAUSEN (J. A.). An Abstract of the whole doctrine of the Christian Religion. *London*, 1804, *8vo* [*The first stereotyped book*]

FRIEDLANDER (Gottlieb). Beiträge zur Buchdruckergeschichte Berlins. *Berlin*, 1834, *8vo*

FRITSCH (Ahasuerus). Abhandlungen von denen Buchdruckern, Buchhändlern, Papiermachern und Buchbindern, insonderheit von deren Statuten, Freyheiten, Streitigkeiten, der Bücher-Censor, Inspection derer Buchdruckereyen-und Buchläden, Ordnungen, &c. *Regensburg*, 1750, *4º*

FRITSCH (A.). Dissertationes duæ historico-politicæ, altera de Abusibus Typographiæ tollendis, altera de Zygenorum, Origine, vita ac moribus. *Jenæ*, 1664, *4to*

FRITSCH (A.). Tractatus de Typographis, Bibliopolis, Chartariis et Bibliopegis, in quo de eorum statutis et immunitatibus abusibus item et controversiis, censura librorum, inspectione typographiarum et bibliopoliorum, ordinatione taxæ, etc. *Jenæ*, 1675, *4to*

FRITSCH (Friedrich). Geschichte der Buckdruckerkunst. Ein kleines Denkmal, den Koryphäen derselben. *Nordhausen*, 1840, *12mo*

FRITZ (G.). Taschenbuch für Buchdrucker. *Magdeburg*, 1854, *4º*

FROEBEL (G.). Album zur vierten Säcularfeier der Erfindung der Buchdruckerkunst und zur Jubelfeier fünfzigjähriger Wirksamkeit der Herren

Buchdrucker: Johann Ludwig Knote, Johann Christoph Wilhelm Esefelder, Friedrich Rudolf Gehring, Johann Ernst Henneberg. *Rudolstadt*, 1840, *8vo*

FRY (Edmund). Pantographia; containing accurate copies of all the known Alphabets in the world, with an English explanation of the peculiar force or power of each Letter; to which are added specimens of all well-authenticated Oral Languages; forming a comprehensive digest of Phonology. *London*, 1799, *royal 8vo*

FRY (E.). Specimen of Modern Printing Types by Edmund Fry, Letter Founder to the King and Prince Regent, Type Street, London. 1816, 8º Another, 1824, 8º

FRY (E.). Specimen of Modern Printing Types. *London*, 1827, *8vo*

FRY and STEELE. A Specimen of Printing Types. *London*, 1794, *royal 8vo*

FUGGER (Jean George). De l'Origine et des Productions de l'Imprimerie primitive. *Paris*, 1759, 8º

FUMAGALLI (Carlo). Dei primi libri a stampa in Italia, e specialmente di un Codice Sublacense impresso avanti il Lattanzio e finora creduto posteriore, discorso. *Lugano*, 1875, *8vo*

FURSTENAU (J. H.). De Initiis Typographiæ Physiologicis Dissertatio. *Rintelii*, 1740, 4º

FUST der Erfinder der Buchdruckerkunst (Drama). *Mainz*, 1792, 8º

GALEOTTI (Melchiorre). Della Tipografia Poliglotta di Propaganda. *Torino*, 1866, *8vo*

GALITZIN (Prince Michel). Deux Xylographies de sa Bibliothèque. *Moscow*, 1864, *8vo* 4 *plates.* 12 *copies only printed*

GALLIZIOLI (Giovambatista). Dell' Origine della Stampa e degli Stampatori di Bergamo. *Bergamo*, 1786, *8vo*

Gama (J. P.). Esquisse historique de Gutenberg. *Paris*, 1857, 8º

Gand (Michel Joseph de). Recherches Historiques et Critiques sur la vie et les éditions de Thierry Martens (Martinus, Mertens). *Alost*, 1845, 8vo

Gandellini (Giovanni Gori). Notizie istoriche degli Intagliatori, 3 vols. *Siena*, 1808, 8vo Notizie degli Intagliatori, raccolte da varj scrittori ed aggiunte a G. G. Gandellini dal Luigi de Angelis, 12 vols. *Siena*, 1808-16, 8vo

Gando (Nicolas). Epreuve des Caractères de la Fonderie de Nicolas Gando. *Paris*, 1745, 4º

Gando (N.). Observations sur le Traité historique et critique: "Sur l'origine et les progrès des caractères de fonte pour l'impression de la musique," par Fournier le Jeune. *Berne*, 1765, 4º

Gar (Tommaso). Letture di bibliologia fatte nella Regia Università degli studî in Napoli durante il primo semestre del 1865. *Torino*, 1868, 8º

Garnier (J. M.). Histoire de l'Imagerie Populaire et des Cartes à Jouer à Chartres. Suivie de Recherches sur le commerce du Colportage des Complaints, Canards, et Chansons des rues. *Chartres*, 1869, 8vo

Garnier Dubourgneuf (J. A.). Code de la Presse. *Paris*, 1822, 8vo

Gaubert. Rénovation de l'Imprimerie. Nouvelle Puissance de la Mécanique. Notice sur la Gérotype ou Machine à distribuer et à composer en Typographie. *Paris*, 1843, 8º

Gaullieur (E. H.). Etudes sur la Typographie Genevoise du XV au XIX siècles, et sur les Origines de l'Imprimerie en Suisse. *Genève*, 1855, 8vo

Gauthier (Toussaint). Histoire de l'Imprimerie en Bretagne. *Rennes*, 1857, 8vo *Only fifty copies printed*

Gauthier (V. Eugene). Annuaire de l'Imprimerie pour 1853. *Paris*, 1853, 8vo

Gauthier-Villars. Imprimerie de Gauthier-Villars, Rue de Seine, Saint-Germain, 10. *Paris*, 1867, 4º

Gautier. Lettre concernant le nouvel art de Graver et d'Imprimer les Tableaux. *Paris*, 1749, 12º

GAZZERA (Costanzo). Notizie intorno all' origine ed al progresso dell' arte Tipografica in Saluzzo. *Saluzzo*, 1831, 8°

GEDENKBUCH an die festlichen Tage der Inauguration des Gutenberg-Denkmals zu Mainz, am 13, 14, 15 und 16 August, 1837. Nebst den Acten, die Entstehung desselben betreffend und einer kurzen Lebensbeschreibung Gutenbergs. *Mainz*, 1837, 8vo

GEDENKBUCH der vierten Säcularfeier der Erfindung der Buchdruckerkunst zu Braunschweig am Johannisfeste des Jahres 1840. *Braunschweig*, 1840, 8vo

GEDENK-BUCH zur IVn Jubelfeier der Erfindung der Buchdruckerkunst zu Franfurt am Main. *Frankfort*, 1840, *royal* 8vo

GEHEIMNISS (Das) des Steindrucks in seinem ganzen Umfange practisch und ohne Rückhalt nach eigenen Erfahrungen. *Tübingen*, 1810, 4to

GENT (Thos.). Life, written by himself, edited by Rev. Joseph Hunter. *London*, 1832, 8vo

GERONVAL (De). Manuel de l'Imprimeur, &c. *Paris*, 1826, 8°

GESCHICHTE der Buchdruckereien der Stadt Leipzig, &c. *Leipzig*, 1840, 8°

GESCHICHTE der Buchdruckerkunst in Basel, &c. *Basel*, 1840, 4°

GESCHICHTE der Buchdruckereien in Kanton St. Gallen. *St. Gallen*, 1840, 8°

GESCHICHTE der Buchdruckereien in Königsberg. *Königsberg*, 1840, 8°

GESCHICHTE der Buchdruckerkunst und ihres Erfinders Johannes Guttenburg. *Berlin*, 1840, 8°

GESCHICHTE der Erfindung der Buchdruckerkunst. *Leipzig*, 1840, 4°

GESCHICHTE. Kritische Geschichte der Buchdruckerkunst. 1780, 4to

GESPRACH, Merkwürdiges, im Reiche der Todten zwischen den ersten Erfindern der Buchdrucker-Kunst, worinne von dem Ursprung, Fortgang und übrigen Schicksalen derselben gehandelt, und insbesondere der Stadt Mayntz der Ruhm von der Erfindung solcher Kunst vindiciret wird: in dem dritten Buchdrucker-Jubilâeo der curiösen welt nebst einigen remarquablen Neuigkeiten aus dem Reiche der Lebendigen mitgetheilet derselben gehandelt wird. *Erfurt*, 1740, 12mo

GESSNER (Chr. Fr.). Die so nöthig als nützlichen Buchdruckerkunst und Schriftgiesserey, mit ihren Schriften, Formaten und allen dazu gehörigen Instrumenten abgebildet auch Klärlich beschrieben, und nebst einer kurzgefassten Erzählung vom Ursprung und Fortgang der Buchdruckerkunst. 4 vols. in 2. *Leipzig*, 1740, 8vo

GESSNER (C. F.). In der Buchdruckerey wohlunterrichteter Lehrjunge, &c. *Leipzig* and *Weimer*, 1743, 8°

GHESQUIERE (J.). Reflexions sur deux pièces relatives à l'histoire de l'Imprimerie publiées dans l'Esprit des Journaux. *Nivelles*, 1780, 8vo

GIARDETTI (Leonardo). Saggio di Caratteri, e fregi della Tipografia. *Firenze*, 1828, 8vo

GIESE (G. C.). Historische Nachricht von der allerersten deutschen Bibelausbabe, welche 1462, zu Mayntz, von Fust und Schoiffhern, gedruckt worden, und in der Bibliothek eines löbl. Gymnasii in Görlitz verwahret wird, am zweyten Jubiläo dieser berühmten Schule, welches auf den 18ten, als am Tage der Uebergabe, und 22sten Juny, als am Tage der Einwehung dieses 1765 sten Jahres einfällt. *Görlitz*, 1765, 12mo

GILIBERTI (Francesco). Studii storici sulla Tipografia, intorno l'origine dell' arte della Stampa. *Palermo*, 1870, 16mo

GILLÉ (J. G.). Manuel de l'Imprimerie, contenant, &c. [*Long list of contents follows.*] Seconde édition, corrigée et augmentée. *Paris*, 1817, 8°

GILLÉ (J. G.). Recueil des divers Caractères, Vignettes, Fleurons et Ornemens de la Fonderie et Imprimerie de J. G. G. *Paris*, 1813, *folio*

GINOUX (P. S.). Comptes-faits Typographiques à l'usage des Imprimeurs, &c. *Paris*, 1858, 4°

GINOUX (P. S.). Vade mecum de l'Imprimeur, &c. (*Second edition of preceding work*). *Paris*, 1860, 8°

GIROUDOT. Notice sur les Presses Mécaniques et celles à la Stanhope. *Paris* [1835], 8°

GIULANELLI (Andrea Pietro). Memorie degli Intagliatori moderni in pietre dure, cammei, e gioie. *Livorno*, 1753, 4to

GIULANI (Nicolo). Notizie della Tipografia Ligure sinoatutto il secolo XVI. *Genova*, 1869, 8vo 22 *plates*

GIULANI (N.) e BELGRANO (L. T.). Supplemento alle Notizie della Tipografia Ligure. *Genova*, 1870, 8º

GIULIARI (G. B. Carlo). Della Tipografia Veronese, saggio storico-letterario. *Verona*, 1871, 8vo *Large paper*

GIUSTI. Intagliatori di legno ed' avorio. *Torino*, 1869, 8º

GIUSTINIANI (Lorenzo). Saggio storico-critico sulla Tipografia del regno di Napoli. *Napoli*, 1793, 4º

GOEBEL (Theodor). Ueber den Satz des Englischen mit besonderer Berücksichtigung der Theilung der Worte. Für Correctoren und Setzer. *Leipzig*, 1865, 12mo

GOETZE (Johann Melchior). Versuch einer Historie der gedruckten Niedersachsischen Bibeln vom Jahr 1470 bis 1621. *Halle*, 1775, 4to

GOETZE (Ludwig). Aeltere geschichte der Buchdruckerkunst in Magdeburg. 1 Abtheitung. Die Drucker das XV. Jahrhunderts. *Magdeburg*, 1872, 8vo 5 *plates*. *All published*. *Only* 120 *copies printed*

GOTTWALD (Eduard). Betrachtungen eines Buchdruckers an Guttenberg's Denkmale, und des Meisters Traum. Gedichte. *Dresden*, 1840, 8vo

GOTTWALD (E.). Erinnerungsblätter an die vierte Säcularfeier der Erfindung der Buchdruckerkunst zu Dresden. *Dresden*, 1840, 8vo *Portraits*

GRAFFER (F.). Die Buchhandel in verbindung mit der Buchdruckerkunst historisch betrachtet. *Wien*, 1813, 8º

GRAHAM (John). Compositor's Text-Book: or, Instructions in the Elements of the Art of Printing, comprising an Essay on Punctuation. *Glasgow*, 1848, 12º

GRAPHOTYPE. The Handbook of Graphotype. A practical Guide for Artists and Amateurs. *London* [1874], 8º

GRASSI (Gioachimo). Dell' Università degli Studi in Mondovi, dissertazione—Della Tipografia in Mondovi, dissertazione. 2 vols. *Mondovi*, 1804, 8º

GRESSWELL (William Parr). Annals of Parisian Typography containing an account of the earliest typographical establishments of Paris, and notices and illustrations of the most remarkable productions of the Parisian Gothic Press; compiled principally to show its general character, and its particular influence upon the early English Press. *London*, 1818, 8vo *Portrait of Guernich, Prototypographer of Paris*

GRESSWELL (W. P.). A view of the Early Parisian Greek Press; including the lives of the Stephani, &c. 2 vols. *Oxford*, 1833, 8vo

GRIMONT (Ferd.). Manuel Annuaire de l'Imprimerie et de la Librairie. *Paris*, 1855, 8vo

GROSSMAN (C. G. L.). Predigt zur vierten Säcularfeier der Erfindung der Buchdruckerkunst am Johannistage 1840. *Leipzig*, 1840, 8vo

GROTEFEND (C. L.). Geschichte der Buchdruckereien in den Hannoverschen und Braunschweigischen Landen. *Hannover*, 1840, 4to

GUETLE (Johann Conrad). Kunst, in Kupfer zu Stechen, zu Radiren und zu Aezen, in schwarzer Kunst und punktirter Manier zu arbeiten. Ehemals durch Abraham Bosse etwas davon herausgegeben, jetzo aberganz neu bearbeitet und mit den neuesten Erfindungen der heutigen Künstler beschrieben, zur Belehrung für angehende Künstler und Liebhaber. 3 vols. *Nürnberg und Altdorf*, 1795-6, 8º

GUICHARD (J. Marie). Notice sur le Speculum Humanæ Salvationis. *Paris*, 1840, 8vo

GUIGNES (Joseph de). Essai Historique sur la Typographie Orientale et Grecque de l'Imprimerie royale. [*Paris*], 1787, 4to

GUIGNES (J. de). Principes de Composition orientale. 1790, 4º

GUSSAGO (Germano Jacopo). Memorie storico-critiche sulla tipografia Bresciana, raccolte ed estese; colle Memorie istorico-critiche delle Bresciane edizioni del Secolo XV e dei libri stampati nel Secolo XV e sul principio del XVI nel' agro Bresciano. *Brescia*, 1811, 4to

GUTCH (John Matthew). Observations or notes upon the Writings of the Ancients, upon the materials which they used, and upon the Introduction of the Art of Printing, etc. *Bristol*, 1827, 8vo *Only 25 copies printed for private distribution*

GUTENBERG. Der geist Johann Gensfleisch's genannt Gutenberg an Dr. C. A. Schaab. *Utrecht*, 1835, 8vo

GUTENBERG, Erfinder der Buchdruckerkunst. Eine historische Skizze mit mehreren Zeichnung und Facsimile. *Strasburg*, 1840, 4to

GUTENBERG à Strasbourg, ou l'Invention de l'Imprimerie. Divertissement en une acte, mêlé de chant et de danses, pour l'inauguration de la statue de Gutenberg. *Strasbourg*, 1840, 8vo

GUTENBERG. Bemerkungen eines Elsassers über die Gutenbergs-Feier, mit besonderer Rücksichtnahme auf die dadurch veraulassten Aeusserungen des Zeitgeistes. *Strassburg, no date*, 8vo

GUTENBERG und die unsterbliche Erfindung der Buchdruckerkunst, sowie deren Vervollkommnung, seit dem Beginn derselben, bis auf unsere zeit; zugleich mit einer kurzen Schilderung derjenigen Manner, welche sich um dieselbe am meisten verdient gemacht haben; mit besonderer Rücksicht auf Deutschland. Eine Festgabe zur vierten Sacularfeier der Erfindung der Buchdruckerkunst den 24. 25. und 26. Juni 1840 allen jüngern und berehren derselben gewidmet. *Leipzig*, 1840, 8vo

GUTENBERG STATUE. Aufruf um das herannahende Sacularfest der Buchdruckerkunst durch Errichtung eines monuments zu Ehren ihres Erfinders Joh. Gensfleisch zum Gutenberg würdig zu feiern. *Mainz*, 1840, 4to

GUTENBERG STATUE. Kurzer Abriss der Lebensbeschreibung Gutenbergs. Nebst nachrichten über die Errichtung und Einweihung seines Denkmals von Thorwaldsen zu Mainz. *Mainz*, 1840, 8vo

GUTENBERGS-ALBUM: zur erinnerung an das Vierte Säcularfest der Erfindung der Buchdruckerkunst, gefeiert zu Ulm. *Ulm*, 1840, 8vo

AARLEM. Catalogus van Voorwerpen ingezonden ter algemeene Typographische Tentoonstelling gehouden te Haarlem, bij gelegenheid der plegtige onthulling van het metallen standbeeld van Lourens Janszoon Coster. [*Haarlem*], 1856, 8vo

HAARLEM. De viering van het vierde Eeuwfeest der Boekdrukkunst te Haarlem, den 10 en 11 Julij 1823. *Haarlem* [1823], 8vo

HAAS (Guillaume). Description et représentation d'une nouvelle Presse d'imprimerie inventée à Basle en 1772. *Basle*, 1791, 4º 3 *plates*

HADDON (John). Specimens of Music Printing. *London*, 1859, 4*to*

HADDON (J.). Specimen Book of Typographical Music

HALL (Charles Carter). The Art of Printing, Historical and Practical: embracing an Outline of the Antecedents, Rise and Progress of the Art, with Brief Biographical Sketches of its Founders. To which is added a concise elementary guide: being a series of practical schemes for the economization of labour. *Sheffield*, 1860, 16º

HALLBAUER (G. C.). De Scriptura et arte Typographiæ. *Jenæ*, 1734, 4º

HALLER (L. A.). Neueste Entdeckung beim Firnissieden der Buchdrucker. *Bern*, 1821, 8º

HALTAUS (Karl). Album Deutscher Schriftsteller zur vierten Säcularfeier der Buchdruckerkunst. *Leipzig*, 1840, 8*vo*

HAMERTON (Philip Gilbert). Etching and Etchers. A new edition, illustrated. *London*, 1876, 8*vo*

HAMMANN (J. M. Herman). Des arts graphiques destinés à multiplier par l'impression, considérés sous le double point de vue historique et pratique. *Genève*, 1857, 12*mo*

HAMMER (Joseph). Ancient Alphabets and Hieroglyphic Characters Explained. *London*, 1806, 4*to*

HANDBOK i Boktryckerikonsten för unga sattare. *Stockholm*, 1853, 8*vo*

HANDBUCH der Buchdruckerkunst, nebst Anweisung, Papiere zu färben. *Berlin*, 1820, 8*vo*

HANDBUCH der Buchdruckerkunst. *Frankfurt am Main*, 1827, 8*vo*

HANDLEIDING tot het corrigeren van drukproeven. *Amsterdam*, 1837, 4*to*

HANDMAID TO THE ARTS. Vol. the First. *London*, 1764, 8*vo* Vol. the Second. Teaching. . . . . II. The art of Engraving, Etching, and scraping Mezzotintos; with the preparation of the aquafortis, varnishes, or other grounds, &c., in the best manner now practised by the French; as also the best manner of printing copper-plates; an improved method of producing washed prints; and of printing in chiaro-oscuro, and with colours, in the way practised by Mr. Le Blon. *London*, 1764, 8vo

HANSARD. Biographical Memoir of Luke Hansard, Esq., many years printer to the House of Commons. [*London*] *not published. Printed by James and Luke G. Hansard and Sons*, 1829, 4to *Portrait*

HANSARD (Thomas Curzon). The Art of Printing; its History and Practice from the days of John Gutenberg. *Edinburgh*, 1851, 8vo

HANSARD (T. C.). The Art of Printing, and Caxton. *London*, 1855, 18º

HANSARD (T. C.). The History of the Art of Printing, &c. *Edinburgh*, 1840, 8º

HANSARD (T. C.). Treatises on Printing and Typefounding, from the seventh edition of the Encyclopædia Britannica. *Edinburgh*, 1841, 12º

HANSARD (T. C.). Typographia: an Historical Sketch of the Origin and Progress of the Art of Printing; with Practical Directions for conducting every department in an Office: with a description of Stereotype and Lithography. Illustrated by engravings, biographical notices and portraits. *London*, 1825, *royal 8vo Largest paper*

HARPEL (Oscar H.). Typograph; or book of Specimens, containing Useful Information, Suggestions, and a collection of examples of Letterpress Job Printing, arranged for the assistance of Master Printers, Amateurs, Apprentices, and others. *Cincinnati*, 1870, *royal 8vo*

HARPEL (O. H.). The Poets and Poetry of Printerdom. *Cincinnati*, 1875, 8vo

HARLESS (C. F.). Die Litteratur der ersten hundert Jahre nach der Erfindung der Typographie in den meisten Hauptfachern der wissenschaften. *Leipzig*, 1840, 8vo

HARPER. Typographical Establishment at New York. *London*, 1855, 8º

HASPER (W.). Handbuch der Buchdruckerkunst. *Carlsruhe*, 1835, 8vo

HASPER (W.). Kurzes practisches Handbuch der Buchdruckerkunst in Frankreich. *Carlsruhe*, 1828, 8vo

HASSE (F. C. A.). Kurze Geschichte der Leipziger Buchdruckerkunst, im verlaufe ihres vierten Jahrhunderts. Einladungschrift der Universität Leipzig zu der bei der vierten Säcularfeier der Buchdruckerkunst von ihr veranstalteten Feierlichkeit. *Leipzig*, 1840, 8vo

HASSE (F. C. A.). Rector Academiæ Orationem in Solemnibus Typographiæ Secularibus IV. Lipsiæ d. xxv. m. Junii h. x. MDCCCXL. *Lipsiæ*, 1840, 4to

HASSE (F. C. A.). Typographia Lipsiensis, impr. saec. quarti, historiæ brevis adumbratis. *Lipsiæ*, 1840, 4º

HASSLER (Conrad Dieterich). Ulm's Buchdruckerkunst mit mehreren artistichen Beilagen. (*Second title*): Die Buchdrucker-Geschichte Ulm's zur vierten Säcularfeier der Erfindung der Buchdruckerkunst. Mit neuen Beiträgen zur Culturgeschichte, dem Faksimile eines der ältesten Drucke und artistischen Beilagen, besonders zur Geschichte der Holzschneidekunst. *Ulm*, 1840, 4to *Plates*

HAUSIUS (Karl Gottlob). Biographie Herren Joh. Gottlob Immanuel Breitkopfs. Ein geschenk sür seine Freunde. [*Leipzig*, 1794] 8vo *Portrait in title*

HEIDELBERG. Zum Gedächtniss der vierten Säcularfeier der Erfindung der Buchdruckerkunst zu Heidelberg am 24. Junius 1840. *Heidelberg*, 1840, 8vo

HEINECKEN (Le Baron). Idée Générale d'une Collection complette d'Estampes, avec une dissertation sur l'Origine de la Gravure. *Leipsic et Vienna*, 1771, 8vo

HEINEMANN (E.). Collection à vendre de Monumens Typographiques. *Offenbach*, 1840, 8vo

HEINLEIN (Heinrich). Festgabe zur vierten Säcularfeier der Erfindung der Buchdruckerkunst. *Leipzig*, 1840, 8vo

HELBIG (H.). Notes et Dissertations relatives à l'Histoire de l'Imprimerie. *Bruxelles* [1863], royal 8vo

HELLER (Joseph). Geschichte der Holzschneidekunst. *Bamberg*, 1823, 8vo

HELLER (J.). Leben Georg Ellinger's, Buchdruckers und Formschneiders zu Bamberg, nebst einer vollstandigen Aufzahlung und Beschreibung seiner sammtlichen gedruckten Schriften und Holzschnitte. Ein Beitrag zur Geschichte der Typographie und als Erganzung der Werke von Panzer, Sprenger und Bartsch. *Bamberg*, 1837, 8vo

HELLER (J.). Praktisches Handbuch für Kupferstichsammler, oder Lexicon der vorzüglichsten und beliebtesten Kupferstecher, Formschneider und Lythographen. 2 vols. *Bamberg, 1823—25, 12mo*

HELLER (J.). Lexicon für Kupferstichsammler über die Monogrammisten, Xylographieen, Niello, Galleriewerke, nebst Berichtigungen und Zusatze zum 1ten und 2ten Theil des Praktischen Handbuches für Kupferstichsammler. *Bamberg, 1838, 12mo*

HELLER (J.). Versuch über das Leben und die Werke Lucas Cranach's. *Bamberg, 1821, 8vo*

HELLER (J. B.). Wohlgemeinte Gedancken über Führung einer Buchdruckerey. *Erfurth, 1740, 8°*

HELLER and ROHM. Die drei Tage der Enthüllungsfeier des Gutenberg-Monuments am 14., 15. und 16. August 1837. Aufgefasst von einem Frankfurter Typographen. Mit Vorwort, vollstandigen Festreden und Anhang. Zum Besten des Gutenberg-Monuments. *Frankfurt am Main* [1837], *8vo*

HELMSCHROTT (Joseph Maria). Verzeichniss alter Druckdenkmale der Bibliothek des Uralten Benediktiner-Stifts zum H. Mang in Füessen, mit literarischen Anmerkungen. 2 *parts. Ulm, 1790, 4to*

HEN (C.). Journal de l'Imprimerie et de la Librairie en Belgique, etc. 5 vols. in 4. *Bruxelles, 8°*

HENNING (Eduard). Erlebnisse des Buchdruckers P. Petersen während seines 10 jahrigen Aufenthalts in Afrika. *Kiel, 1851, 8vo*

HENRICI (Dr. G.) Die Buchdruckerkunst, nach ihrem Einflusse auf Wissenschaft, Religion, Gesittung und bürgerlichen Verkehr. *Braunschweig, 1849, 8vo*

HENRICY (Ant.). Notice sur l'origine de l'Imprimerie en Provence. *Aix, 1826, 8°* *Reprinted from the* "*Mémoires de la Société académique d'Aix*"

HENRY (J.). Dialogue entre une Presse Mécanique et une Presse à Bras, etc. *Paris, 1830, 8°*

HENZE (A.). Handbuch der Schriftgiesserei und der verwandten Nebenzweige. *Weimar, 1844, 8°*

HERBERGER (Theodor). Augsburg und seine frühere Industrie. *Augsburg, 1852, 8vo*

HERLUISON (Henri). Plan d'une Bibliothèque Orléanaise ou Essai de Bibliographie Locale. *Orléans, 1868, 8vo* 100 *copies printed*

HERLUISON (H.). Recherches sur les Imprimeurs et Libraires d'Orléans. *Orléans*, 1868, 8*vo*

HERMANN (Godof.). Oratio in quartis festis secularibus artis Typographicæ. *Lipsiæ*, 1840, 4*to*

HESSE (L. A. C.). Epreuves d'impression satinée, par L. A. C. Hesse à Amsterdam, 1806, 4*to*

HEUBNER (Gustav). Das vereinigte Gutenbergs und Turnfeste der Stadt Plauen am 24. Juni 1840 beschrieben und nebst den dabei gehaltenen Reden und gefungenen Liedern. *Plauen* [1840] 8*vo*

HILARIA TYPOGRAPHICA ERFORDIENSIA, das ist Historischer vericht von der Jubel-Feyer in 1740. *Erfurt*, [1740], 4*to*

HILDEBRANDT (J. C.). Handbuch für Buchdrucker, &c. *Eisenach*, 1835, 8º

HINLOPEN (F. C.). De uitvinding der Boekdrukkunst. *Haarlem*, 1856, 8*vo*

HIRSCHFELD (J. B.). Schrift Proben der Buchdruckerei von. *Leipzig*, 1826, 4*to*

HISTOIRE de l'invention de l'Imprimerie par les monuments. [*By* E. Duverger.] *Paris*, 1840, 4*to*

HISTORY and Art of Ingraving. *London*, 1747, 12*mo*

HODGSON (Thomas). An essay on the origin and progress of Stereotype Printing; including a description of the various processes. *Newcastle*, 1820, 8*vo*   306 *copies printed*

HOECHEL (C. H.). Das Heroen der Kunstliche Gemalde der ausgezeichnetsten Typographen früherer Zeit. *Ulm*, 1836, 8º

HOFFMANN (C.) und WEITHAS. C. Hoffmanns Buchdruckerpresse von Gusseisen. *Leipzig*, 1826, 8º

HOFFMANN (F. L.). Description d'une édition de quelques dialogues de Lucien, traduit en latin par Érasme, imprimée à Louvain, en 1512, par Thierry-Martens. [*Bruxelles*, 1859], 8*vo Twenty-five copies reprinted from the "Bulletin du Bibliophile Belge"*

HOFFMANN (F. L.). Essai d'une Liste chronologique des ouvrages et dissertations concernant l'Histoire de l'Imprimerie en Belgique et en Hollande. *Bruxelles*, 1859, 8*vo Only thirty copies reprinted from the "Bulletin du Bibliophile Belge"*

HOFFMANN (F. L.). Essai d'une liste des ouvrages concernant l'Histoire de l'Imprimerie en Italie. *Bruxelles*, 1852, 8º   150 *copies printed separately from the "Bulletin du Bibliophile Belge," tome* 9

HOFFMANN (F. L.). Lettres et publications de H. Agileus de Bois-le-Duc (1503-1595). *Bruxelles*, 1863, 8º

HOFFMANN (F. L.). Versuch einer Bibliographie der Geschichte der Buchdruckerkunst in Dänemark und in Schweden und Norwegen. *Dresden*, 1861, 8º *Only 100 copies printed from the "Neuern Anzeiger für Bibliographie"*

HOFFMANN (F. L.). Verzeichniss von Schriften welche die Geschichte der Buchdruckerkunst in der Schweiz zur Gegenstand haben. *Halle*, 8º

HOFFMANN (Gottfried Daniel). Von denen ältisten Kayserlichen und Landesherrlichen Bucher-Druckoder Verlag-Privilegien, [*no place*], 1777, 12mo

HOFFMAN (John Daniel). De Typographiis eorumque Initiis et Incrementis in Regno Poloniæ et Magno Ducatu Lithuaniæ, cum Variis Observationibus Rem Litterariam et Typographicam utriusque gentis, aliquâ ex parte Illustrantibus. *Dantisci*, 1740, 4to

HOIER (A.). Programmata II. de Originibus Typographiæ. *Sleswig*, 1740, 4º

HOLLOWAY (Thomas). Memoir of the late Mr. Thomas Holloway, by one of his executors: and most respectfully dedicated to the subscribers to the engravings from the Cartoons of Raphael. *London. Printed for the author*, 1827, 8vo

HOLMES (John). A descriptive Catalogue of the Books in the Library of John Holmes. With notices of authors and printers. 5 vols. *Norwich*,[*privately printed*], 1828-40, 8vo

HOLTROP (J. W.). Monuments Typographiques des Pays Bas au XV siècle. *La Haye*, 1868, 4to

HOLTROP (J. W.). Thierry Martens d'Alost. Etude bibliographique. *La Haye*, 1867, 8vo

HOLTZAPFFEL and Co. Printing Apparatus for the use of Amateurs. *London*, 1846, 8vo

HORNE (T. H.). Introduction to the Study of Bibliography. 2 vols. *London*, 1814, 8vo

HORNSCHUCH (H.). Der bey Buchdruckereyen wohlunterwiesene Corrector. *Frankfurt und Leipzig*, 1739, 8º

HOUBLOUP. Théorie Lithographique. *Paris*, 1825, 8º

HOUDRY. Ars Typographica Carmen. 4º

HOUGHTON (T. S.). The Printer's Practical Everyday Book, calculated to assist the young printer to work with ease and expedition. *London*, 1841, 12º

HOYOIS (E.). Notice sur Josse Bade. *Mons*, (c. 1850). 8º

HUBAUD (L. J.). Examen Critique d'un Opuscule intitulé : " Quelques Recherches sur les Débuts de l'Imprimerie à Toulouse," par M. Desbarreaux-Bernard, extrait des Mémoires de l'Académie des Sciences, Inscriptions, et Belles-Lettres de Toulouse. *Marseille*, 1858, 8vo

HUBAUD (L. J.). Examen Critique d'un Nouvel Opuscule de M. le Docteur Desbarreaux-Bernard, intitulé : " L'Imprimerie à Toulouse aux XVᵉ, XVIᵉ, et XVIIᵉ Siècles." *Marseille*, 1866, 8vo

HUBER (Michael). Notices générales des Graveurs, divisés par Nations, et des Peintres, rangés par Ecoles. Précédés de l'Histoire de la Gravure et de la Peinture depuis l'Origine de ces Arts jusqu'à nos jours, et suivies d'un Catalogue raisonné d'une collection choisie d'Estampes. *Dresde*, 1787, 8º

HULLMANDEL (C.). The Art of Drawing on Stone; giving a full explanation of the various styles, the different methods to be employed to ensure success, the modes of correcting and the several causes of failure. *London*, 1835, 8º 9 *lithographic plates*

HULLMANDEL (C.) Specimens of Lithography. *London*, 1829, 4º

HULST (Felix van). Christophe Plantin. *Liége*, 1846, 8vo

HULTMAN (C. G.) Bibliographische Zeldzaamheden. *'s Hertogenbosch*, 1818, 8vo

HUMBERT (Major de). Abrégé Historique de l'Origine et des Progrèz de la Gravure et des Estampes en Bois et en Taille Douce. *Berlin*, 1752, 12º

HUMPHREYS (Henry Noel). A History of the Art of Printing, its invention and progress to the Middle of the Sixteenth Century. *London*, 1868, *impl.* 4to *Plates of facsimiles from Block-Books, and important Typographical Monuments of Germany, Holland, Italy, France, England, &c. including facsimiles of the Press of Caxton, Wynkyn de Worde, Pynson, &c.*

HUMPHREYS (H. N.). Masterpieces of the Early

Printers and Engravers. *London*, 1870, *folio.* Large paper

HUPFAUER (Paul). Druckstücke aus dem XV Jahrhunderte. *Augsburg*, 1794, 12mo 23 *plates*

ICELAND. Söguágrip um Prentsmidjur og Prentara á Islandi. Reykjavík. 1867, 12º

IHM (B. A.). Der bunten Farben in der Buchdruckerei, &c. *Biel*, 1865, 8º

IMBERT (D. G.) Dissertation sur l'origine de l'Imprimerie en Angleterre. *Paris*, 1775, 8vo

IMPRIMERIE IMPERIALE (*de Russie*). Echantillons des Caractères. *St. Petersbourg*, 1790, *sm.* 8vo

INVENTION de l'Imprimerie à Strasbourg par J. Gutenberg. *Strasbourg*, 1840, 8º

INVENZIONE (Dell') della stampa e delle più celebri tipografie Italiane. *Adria*, 1872, 4º

ISEGHEM (A. F. von). Biographie de Thierry Martens d'Alost, premier Imprimeur de la Belgique, suivie de la Bibliographie de ses éditions. *Malines*, 1852, 8º *Plates*

ISERMANN (A.). Anleitung zur Chemitypie, nach eigenen Erfahrungen. *Leipzig*, 1869, 12mo

ISERMANN (A.). Anleitung zur Stereotypen-Giesserei in Gyps- und Papiermatrizen. *Leipzig*, 1869, 12mo

JAAGER (J. Pluim de). Morgenwandeling van Laurens Janszoon Koster in den Hout bij Haarlem anno 1423, Dichtstukje. *Dordrecht*, 1823, 8vo

JACKSON (John Baptist). An Essay on the invention of Engraving and Printing in Chiaro Oscuro, as practised by Albert Dürer, Hugo di Carpi, &c. and the application of it to the making of Paper Hangings of taste, duration and elegance. *London*, 1754, 4to

JACOB, l'aîné. Idées Générales sur les Causes de l'Anéantissement de l'Imprimerie et sur la nécessité de rendre à cette Profession, ainsi qu'à celle de la Libraire, le rang honorable qu'elles ont toujours tenu l'une et l'autre parmi les Arts Libéraux. *Orléans*, 1806, 8º

JACOB (J. L. C.). Aanteekeningen over het geslacht en de drukwerken van den Delftschen boekdrukker Hermanus Schinckel. *'s Gravenhage*, 1843, sm. 8vo *Not printed for sale*

JACOB (J. L. C.). Bonavetuur en Abraham Elzevier, kleine letterkundige bijdrage. *'s Hage*, 1841, 12mo facsimile. *Printed on pink paper, not for sale*

JACOB (P. L.). Curiosités de l'histoire des arts. Notice sur le parchemin et le papier; recherches sur les cartes à jouer; origine de l'imprimerie; la reliure depuis l'antiquité jusqu'à dix-septième siècle; histoire de l'orfèvrerie Française; les instruments du musique au moyen âge. *Paris*, 1858, 16mo

JACOBACCI (Vinc.). Orazione funebre in morte del Cavalier G. B. Bodoni. *Parma*, 1814, 8º

JAECK (Heinrich Joachim). Denkschrift für das Jubelfest der Buchdruckerkunst zu Bamberg, am 24 Juni 1840, als Spiegel der allseitigen Bildungs-Verhalltnisse seit unserer geschichtlichen Periode. *Erlangen*, 1840, 8vo *Portrait*

JAMES (Sir Henry). On Photo-Zincography and other Photographic Processes employed at the Ordnance Survey Office, Southampton. *London*, 1862, 4º

JANSEN (G.). Mittheilungen für Buchdrucker und Schriftgiesser. *Berlin*, 1852-4, 4º

JANSEN (Henri). Essai sur l'Origine de la Gravure en Bois et en Taille Douce, et sur la Connoissance des Estampes des XVe et XVIe siècles, où il est parlé aussi de l'origine des Cartes à Jouer et des Cartes Géographiques; suivi de recherches sur l'Origine du Papier de Coton et de Lin; sur la Calligraphie, depuis les plus anciens manuscrits; sur les Filigranes des Papiers des XIVe, XVe et XVIe Siècles; ainsi que sur l'Origine et le premier Usage des Signatures et des Chiffres dans l'art de la Typographie. 2 vols. *Paris*, 1808, 8vo. *Plates*

JENA. Kurtze Nachricht wie die Buchdruckergesellschaft zu Jena in 1740 ihr 3s Jubelfest gefeyert hat. *Jena*, 1740, 4to

JOCISCUS (A.). Oratio de ortu, vita et obitu Joannis Oporini Basil., typographicorum Germaniæ principis. Acced. librorum per Joan. Oporinum excusorum catalogus. *Argentorati*, 1569, 8°

JOHNSON (Edmund C.). Tangible Typography, or how the blind read. *London*, 1853, 8vo

JOHNSON (Henry). An Introduction to Logography. 1783, 8°

JOHNSON (John). Typographia, or the Printers' Instructor: including an Account of the Origin of Printing, with Biographical Notices of the Printers of England, from Caxton to the Close of the Sixteenth Century; a Series of Ancient and Modern Alphabets, and Domesday Characters; together with an Elucidation of Every Subject connected with the Art. 2 vols. *London*, 1824, *royal 8vo, woodcuts. Printed on three sizes, the largest, in royal 8vo, being called* " Roxburgh Copies "

JOHNSON. An Abridgment of Johnson's "Typographia," or the Printers' Instructor, with an Appendix. *Boston*, 1828, 12mo

JONES (H. G.). Andrew Bradford, the founder of the Newspaper Press in America. An Address before the Historical Society of Pennsylvania, February 9, 1869. *Philadelphia*, 1869, 8vo

JONES (John Winter). Observations upon the Discovery of two rare Tracts in the Library of the British Museum, hitherto unknown, from the Press of William Caxton. Communicated to the Society of Antiquaries in a letter to Sir Henry Ellis. *London*, 1846, 4° *Reprinted from "Archæologia," vol.* xxxi. *pp.* 412-424.

JOURNAL für Buchdruckerkunst, Schriftgiesserei und die verwandten Fächer. Herausgegeben von Johann Heinrich Meyer. *Braunschweig*, 1834, 4to *In progress*

JOURNAL Général de l'Imprimerie et de la Librairie, Nos. 1-44, 1810-11; continued as:—
Bibliographie de l'Empire Français; tom. 1-3, 1811-13; continued as:—
Bibliographie de la France, ou Journal Général de l'Imprimerie et de la Librairie; tom. 4-45, 1813-56; continued as:—
Journal Général de l'Imprimerie et de la Librairie, deuxième série, tom. 1, &c. 8vo *In progress*

JOURNAL typographique et bibliographique, commencé en 1797 par le Doct. Roux, &c. 13 vols. *Paris*, 1797-1810, 8°

JUBELZEUGNISSE, Oeffentliche, welche bey dem von einigen Buchdruckern zu Halle den 25. Jul. 1740 Erneuerten Andenken der vor dreyhundert Jahren erfundenen Buchdruckerkunst von der Hochlöbl. Friedrichsuniversität und andern gelehrten gönnern feyerlichst abgeleget worden. *Halle,* 1741, 4*to*

JUBILÆUM Typographorum Lipsiensium : oder zweyhundert-Jähriges Buchdrucker Jubel Fest, wie solches deroselben Kunst-Verwandte zu Leipzig, am Tage Johannis des Tauffers, anno Christi, 1640, und also gleich 200. Jahr nach Erfindung dieser edlen kunst, mit Christlichen Ceremonien celebriret und begangen, &c. [*Leipzig*], 1640, 4*to*

JUBILAUMS-Buchlein, oder Geschichte, wie die Buchdruckerkunst in Deutschland erfunden worden ist, nebst Ander'm, was dazu gehört. Erzahlt für's Volk und für Freunde des Volkes. *Mannheim,* 1840, 12*mo*

JUDEX (Matthaeus). De Typographiæ Inventione et de Prelorum Legitima Inspectione. *Copenhagen,* 1566, 8*vo*

JULIEN (Stanislas). Documents sur l'Art d'Imprimer à l'aide de planches en bois . . . inventé en Chine bien longtemps avant que l'Europe en fît usage [*extract from Journal*]. 1847, 8*vo*

JULLIERON (N.). Thrésor de l'Imprimerie, démonstré par la Multitude et Diversité de ses Caractères. *Lyon,* 1622, 4º

JUNGENDRES (S. J.). Disquisitio in notas Characteristicas Librorum a Typographiæ Incunabulo ad an. MD. impressorum. Ex antiquissimis Codicibus investigatas et rarissimorum Scriptorum recensione confirmatas. In Jubilæi Typographici tertii mnemosynon conscripta. *Norimbergæ,* 1740, 4º

JUNIUS (Hadrian). Batavia. In qua præter gentis et insulæ antiquitatem, originem, decora, mores, aliaque ad eam historiam pertinentia, declaratur quæ fuerit vetus Batauia, quæ Plinio, Tacito et Ptolemæo cognita : quæ item genuina inclytæ Francorum nationis fuerit sedes. *Lugduni Batavorum,* 1588, 4*to* (*Pp.* 253-257 *contain the statement, made for the first time, and the origin of so much controversy, that Typography was invented by Koster at Haarlem*)

K (G.). Die 400 jahrige Jubelfeier der Erfindung der Buchdruckerkunst in Leipzig am 24.25.26 Juni, 1840. *Camenz*, 1840, 8vo

KADE (E.). Die 4e Säcularfeier der Buchdruckerkunst zu Leipzig, 1840. *Leipzig*, 1841, 4to

KAUTZ (K. F. F. O. von). Ueber die wahre Epoche der eingeführten Buchdruckerkunst zu Wien. *Wien*, 1784, f⁰

KELCHNER (Ernst). Die Buchdruckerei und ihre Druckwerke zu Ober-Ursel. *Wiesbaden*, 1863, 8vo

KIESEWETTER (Dr. L.). Gedränkte Geschichte der Buchdruckerkunst von ihrer Erfindung bis auf unsere Tage. *Glogau*, 1840, sm. 8vo

KINGSTON (W.). System of Printing in Dry Colours. *London*, 12⁰

KIRCHER (E. W. G.). Anweisung in der Buchdruckerkunst so viel davon das Drucken betrifft. *Braunschweig*, 1793, 12mo

KLEMM (Heinrich). Die Planotypie, ihre Entstehung und Verwerthung zu typographischen, merkantilen und gewerblichen Zwecken. *Dresden*, 1871, 48⁰

KLEMMEN (J. C.). Das angedencken des Dritten Jubel-Fests der Edlen Buchdrucker-Kunst auf der Universitat Tübingen. *Tübingen*, 1740, 4to

KLIMSCH & BÖHLER. Die Gründformen der gebräuchlichsten Schriften. Heft I. (*query all published*). *Frankfurt* [1870], 4to

KLINDWORTH (C. A.). Kurze Beschreibung der Buchdruckerpressen welche in der Maschinenfabrik von C. A. Klindworth in Hannover angefertigt werden, &c. *Hannover*, 1841, 4⁰

KNAUTH (Chris.). Annales Typographici Lusatiæ Superioris oder Geschichte der Ober-Lausitzischer Buchdruckereyen. *Lauben* [1740], 4to

KNAUTH (C.). Historischer Abriss von dem anfang und Wachsthum der Gelehrsamkeit in Ober-Lausitz, Buchrucker Jubel Festes 1740. *Leipzig* [1740], 4to

KNECHT (M.). Nouveau Manuel Complet du Dessinateur et de l'Imprimeur Lithographe. Nouvelle édition, entièrement réfondue, mise au courant de l'industrie actuelle, et augmentée de plusieurs procédés nouveaux concernant la Lithographie mécanique, la Chromolithographie, la Lithophotographie, la Zincographie et traitant des papiers de sûreté. *Paris*, 1867, 12mo *With Atlas*

KNIGHT (Charles). The Old Printer and the Modern Press. *London*, 1854, 12º

KNIGHT (C.). William Caxton, the first English Printer: a Biography. *London [Knight's Weekly Volume, vol.* 1], 1844, 12º

KNIGHT (Edwd. K.). The First Century of the Republic: Printing (In Harper's Magazine). *New York*, 1875, 8vo

KOBELL (Franz von). Die Galvanographie, eine Methode, gemalte Tuschbilder durch galvanische Kupferplatten im Drucke zu vervielfältigen. *München*, 1842, 4º

KOCH (M.). Kurzgefasste kritische Geschichte der Erfindung der Buchdruckerkunst, &c. *Wien*, 1841, 8º

KÖHLER (G.). Zur Geschichte der Buchdruckerei in Görlitz. *Görlitz*, 1840, 4º

KÖHLER (J. D.). Hochverdiente und aus bewährten Urkunden wohlbeglaubte Ehren-Rettung Johann Guttenbergs. *Leipzig*, 1741, 4to

KÖRK (F. X.). Wichtige Erfindung einer einfachen nicht zu Kostspieligen Druckmaschine auf Papp- und Tafeldruck. *Landsh.* 1853, 8º

KOHELL (F. von). Die Galvanographie. *München*, 1846, 8º

KONING (Jacobus). Aan den Heer G. van Lennep over deszelfs Aanmerkingen wegens een' Houten Druk-vorm. *Amsterdam* (1809), 8vo

KONING (J.). Beantwoording van het nader geschrift van den Heer Mr. G. van Lennep over den houten druk-vorm, den 29sten van Grasmaand 1809, te Leyden, verkscht. [*Amsterdam*, 1809], 8vo

KONING (J.). Bijdragen tot de Geschiedenis der Boekdrukkunst. *Haarlem*, 1818, 8vo—Tweede Stuk (*2nd part*). *Haarlem*, 1820, 8vo

KONING (J.). De Druk-kunst eene verhandeling uitgesprooken in eene aanzienlyke maatschappy. *Amsterdam*, 1794, 8vo

KONING (J.). Dissertation sur l'Origine, l'Invention et le Perfectionnement de l'Imprimerie. Traduite du Hollandois. *Amsterdam*, 1819, 8vo

KONING (J.). In welk jaar dezer eeuw behoort het

vierde Jubel van de uitvinding der Boekdruk-kunst te Haarlem gevierd te worden? In twee Brieven van den heere J. Koning te Amsterdam, aan den wel eerw. heere A. de Vries te Haarlem, beantwoord. *Haarlem*, 1822, 8vo

KONING (J.). Verhandeling over de uitvinding der boekdrukkunst der Koster. 1815, 8vo [*An extract*]

KONING (J.). Verhandeling over den oorsprong de uitvinding, verbetering en volmaking der boekdrukkunst. *Haarl.* 1816, 8vo

KONING (J.). Vier brieven gewisseld tusschen J. Scheltema en J. K. *Haarlem*, 1823, 8vo

KORTEBRANT (Jakob). Lof der Drukkunste, te Haarlem uitgevonden door L. J. Koster. *Delf*, 1740, 4to

KOSTER. Aanmerkingen op de gedenkschriften wegens het vierde eeuwgetijde van de uitvinding der Boekdrukkunst, door Lourens Janszoon Koster, overgenomen uit de s' Gravenhaagsche Couranten van den 12, 14, en 28 Julij 1824 en vermeerderd met eenige aanteekeningen, strekkende om aan te toonen dat door dit werk aan de zaak van Haarlem nadeel is toegebragt. *'s Gravenhage*, 1824, 8vo

KOSTER. Bewijzen voor de echteid en gelijkenis der oude afbeeldingen van Coster. *Haarlem*, 1847, 8vo

KOSTER. De Commissie tot onderzoek naar het jaar der uitvinding van de Boekdrukkunst. (*Harlem*), 1822, 8vo

KOSTER. Haarlems en Kosters regt op de uitvinding der Boekdrukkunst. [*Harlem*, 1823, 8vo]

KOSTER. Het vierde Eeuwgetijde van de Uitvinding der Boekdrukkunst, gevierd den 10den van Hooimaand, 1823. Door het hornsche departement der Maatschappij: tot nut van 't Algemeen. *Amsterdam*, 1823, 8vo

KOSTER. Korte beschrijving der Boeken door Lourens Janszoon Koster, te Haarlem, tusschen de Jaren 1420 en 1440 gedrukt; alsmede van eenige merkwaardigheden tot de geschiedenis van L. J. Koster betrekkelijk, bij gelegenheid van het vierde Eeuwfeest van de Uitvinding der Boekdrukkunst, in de Kerk der Doopsgezinde Gemeente aldaar ten toon gesteld, op den 10en en 11en Julij, 1823. [*Haarlem*, 1823], 8vo

Koster. Laurens Janszoon Koster. Een Liedje bij de Onthulling van zijn Standbeeld. *Rotterdam*, 1856, 8vo

Koster. Laurens Jansz. Koster. Jaarboekje voor Typographische Vereenigingen. Eerste Jaargang, 1856. *Leyden*, 1856, 12mo

Koster. Laurier-Krans, geologten om 't hoofd van Laurens Koster, eerste Uitvinder der Boekdrukkunst binnen Haarlem. *Haarlem*, 1726, 4to

Koster. Leven van L. Jzn. Koster . . . eerste vinder der drukkunst. *Amst.* 1730, 8º

Koster. Levens-Schets van Laurens Janszoon Koster. [*Part of a book.*] 8vo

Koster. Lotgevallen van Costers Woning. *Haarlem*, 1851, 8vo

Koster. Souvenir en Programma van het Costerfeest te Haarlem, gehouden op 15., 16. en 17. Julij 1856. Met eene gelithographieerde plaat van het metallen standbeeld. *'s Gravenhage*, 1856, 8vo

Koster. Tien vragen van eenen Hoogduitscher . . . eene hulde aan L. J. Koster. *Deventer*, 1856, 8vo

Koster. XII Volks Liedekens op bekende wijzen, ter vervrolijking van Lourens Jansz. Koster's vierde Eeuw—Feest, door Democriet. *Harlem*, 1823, 12mo

Koster. Vrolijke Liederen der Drukkersgezellen te Dordrecht, toegewijd aan het vierde eeuwfeest, van de uitvinding der boekdrukkunst door Laurens Janszoon Koster, gezongen ter gelegenheid van hunnen feestvierenden Optogt, mit eene rijdende en tegelijk werkende Drukpers, des avonds van den 10 Julij 1823 bij Fakkelligt. *Dordrecht*, 1823, 8vo

Koster Commemoration. Beknopt Verhaal van de viering van het Vierde Eeuwgetijde na de vinding der Boekdrukkunst. *Batavia*, 1825, 8vo *Fine paper*

Koster Commemoration. Rapport van de Commissie benoemd door den raad der Stad Haarlem tot het onderzoek naar het jaar van de uitvinding der boekdrukkunst. *Haarlem*, 1822, 8vo

Koster Commemoration, 1856. *A Collection of Programmes, Pamphlets, Songs, Newspapers, &c., &c., relating thereto*

KRAUSE (J. G.).   Apparatus ad Pauli Manutii vitam, pars prior. *Lipsiæ*, 1750, 4º

KRAUSE (L. W.).   Beschreibung der Feier des vierten Säcular-Festes der Erfindung der Buchdruckerkunst in der officinen von L. W. Krause am 21. Juli 1840. Eine Denkschrift für die Theilnehmer des Festes. *Berlin*, 1840, 12mo

KRAUSS (F.) und MALTE (F.). Handbuch für Lithographen und Steindrucker, &c. *Stuttgart*, 1852, 8º

KRUEGER (Gustav). Predigt zur Belehrung seiner Gemeinde über die nahe Feier des vierhundertjährigen Jubelfestes der Buchdruckerkunst am zweiten Pfingstfeiertage gehalten und mit erläuternden geschichtlichen Anmerkungen auf Verlangen in Druck gegeben. *Delitzsch*, 1840, 8vo

KUGELMANN (Joseph). Histoire de l'Imprimerie en Portugal. *Paris*, 1867, 8vo

KULB (Ph. H.).   Geschichte der Erfindung der Buchdruckerkunst. *Mainz*, 1837, 8vo

KUNAD (Jac. Fried.). De Typographiā Disputatio. *Wittemb.*, 1697, 4º

KUNTZ (C.). Die Erfindung der Buchdruckerkunst, ihre ersten Anfänge und ihre Entwicklungen. Nebst einem Berichte über die vierte Säkularfeier dieser Erfindung in Strasburg 1840. Ein Gedenk- und Lesebuchlein für Volk und Schule. *Strasburg*, 1840, 12mo

KUNZEL (Hermann). Die Zurichtung und der Druck von Illustrationen. Kurzer Leitfaden für Maschinenmeister. *Leipzig*, 1867, 4to

KUSTER (G. G.). Historia artis Typographicæ in Marchia. *Berolini*, 1746, 4º

L (S. L.).   Over den Oorsprong der Boekdrukkunst. *Te Groningen*, 1781, 8vo

LABORDE (Léon de). Débuts de l'imprimerie à Strasbourg, ou Recherches sur les travaux mystérieux de Gutenberg dans cette ville, et sur le procès qui lui fut intenté en 1439 à cette occasion. *Paris*, 1840, 8vo

LABORDE (L. de). Histoire de la Gravure en Manière Noire. *Paris*, 1839, *royal* 8*vo*

LABORDE (L. de). Nouvelles Recherches sur l'origine de l'Imprimerie. [*Second title*] Débuts de l'Imprimerie à Mayence et à Bamberg, ou Description des Lettres d'Indulgence du Pape Nicolas V., pro regno Cypri, imprimées en 1454. *Paris*, 1840, *large* 4*to Woodcuts and facsimiles*

LABOULAYE (Ch.). Un Mot sur l'Imprimerie Nationale. *Paris*, 1851, 8*vo*

LABUS (G.). Sulla "Tipografia del secolo XV." dell' abate Giacinto Amati. *Milano*, 1834, 8º

LACAILLE (Jean de). Histoire de l'Imprimerie et de la Librairie, où l'on voit son origine et son progrès jusqu'en 1689. *Paris*, 1689, 4*to*

LACKMAN (Adam Henry). Annalium Typographicorum selecta quædam Capita. *Hamburgi*, 1740, 4*to*

LACROIX (Paul), FOURNIER (Edouard), et SERÉ (Ferd.). Histoire de l'Imprimerie et des Arts et Professions qui se rattachent à la Typographie, comprenant l'Histoire des anciennes Corporations et Confréries d'écrivains, d'enlumineurs, etc. depuis leur fondation jusqu'à leur suppression en 1789. *Paris*, 1852, *impl.* 8*vo*

LAIRE (François Xavier). Ad Abbatem Ugolini fulginatem Epistola Autoris libri cui titulus: Specimen Typographiæ Romanæ. *Argentorati (Paris)*, 1779, 8º

LAIRE (F. X.). De l'Origine et des Progrès de l'Imprimerie en Franche Comté. *Dôle*, 1784, 12*mo*

LAIRE (F. X.). Index Librorum, ab inventa Typographia ad annum 1500, chronologicè dispositus, cum Notis Historiam Typographico-litterariam illustrantibus. 2 vols. *Sens*, 1791, 8*vo*

LAIRE (F. X.). Mémoires pour servir à l'Histoire Littéraire de quelques grands hommes du 15ᵉ Siècle, avec Supplément aux Annales Typographiques de Maittaire. *Naples*, 1778, 8º

LAIRE (F. X.). Specimen Historicum Typographiæ Romanæ XV. Sæculi. *Rome*, 1778, 8*vo*

LALANNE (Maxime). Traité de la Gravure à l'eau-forte, texte et planches. *Paris*, 1866, 8*vo*

LAMARTINE (A. de). Gutenberg, Inventeur de l'Imprimerie (1400-1469). *Paris*, 1853, *sm.* 8º

LAMBINET (P.). Origine de l'Imprimerie, d'après

les titres authentiques, l'opinion de M. Daunou et celle de M. Van Praet. 2 vols. *Paris*, 1810, 8*vo*

LAMBINET (P.). Recherches Historiques, Littéraires et Critiques sur l'origine de l'Imprimerie; particulièrement sur ses premiers établissements au 15e Siècle dans la Belgique, maintenant réunie à la République Française; ornées des Portraits et des Ecussons des premiers Imprimeurs Belges. *Bruxelles*, an vii [1799], 8*vo*

LAMESLE (Claude). Epreuves générales des caractères qui se trouvent chez Claude Lamesle, fondeur de caractères d'imprimerie. *Paris*, 1842, 4*to*

LAMMINGER (M.). Ueber das Firnisssieden der Buchdrucker, &c. *Nuremberg*, 1817, 8°

LANDINE (A. F. de). Histoire abrégée de l'Imprimerie, ou précis sur son origine, son établissement en France, &c. *Paris* [1840], 8*vo* 100 *copies only printed*

LANDSEER (John). Lectures on the Art of Engraving, delivered at the Royal Institution of Great Britain. **London**, 1807, 8*vo*

LANGE (A. P.). Schöffer von Gernsheim der Buchdrucker und Buchhändler. *Leipzig*, 1864, **4to**

LANGENSCHWARZ (Maximilian). De Vergoding van Gutenberg in onze dagen; of tien vragen tot bewijs, dat Johann Gutenberg niet de uitvinder der Boekdrukkunst was. *Groningen*, 1842, 8*vo*

LANGENSCHWARZ (M.). Die Gutenberg-Schwärmerei unsrer Tage. Oder Zehn Fragen als Beweis dass Johann Gutenberg nicht Erfinder der Buchdruckerkunst war. *Leipzig*, 1841, **8°**

LANGLES (L.). Détails Littéraires et Typographiques sur l'Edition du Dictionnaire et des Grammaires Tartares Mantchoux. *Paris*, 1790, 8°

LANGLOIS (E. H.). Essai sur la Calligraphie des Manuscrits du Moyen-Age et sur les Ornements des premiers Livres d'Heures imprimés. *Rouen*, 1841, 8°

LAPPENBERG (J. M.). Zur geschichte der Buchdruckerkunst in Hamburg am 24 Juni, 1840. *Hamburg*, 1840, **4to**

LASALETTE (P. J.). Sténographie Musicale, ou Manière Abrégée d'écrire la Musique, à l'usage des Compositeurs et des Imprimeurs. *Paris*, 1805, 8°

LASTEYRIE (le Cᵉ. C. P. de). 'typographie 'economique ou l'art d'imprimerie mis à la portée de tous. '*paris*, 1837, 8*vo*

LAWSHER (F. C.). Die Lithographische Hochätzkunst, oder die Kunst auf Kalkschiefer oder Marmorstein durch Säuren so erhaben zu ätzen, dass es wie Bleitypen abgedruckt werden kann. Nebst einer gründlichen Anleitung, von diesen hochglätzen Lithographieen Stereotypen abnehmen zu können. Eine höchst wichtige Erfindung für den Buchdruck, als billigeres Surrogat für den theuern Holzschnitt und dessen Abklatschplatten. *Baltimore, Ind.* 1835, 8º

LECHI (Luigi). Della Tipografia Bresciana nel Secolo Decimoquinto. *Brescia,* 1854, 4to *Only 208 copies printed, five on large paper*

LEDEBOER (A. M.). De boekdrukkers, boekverkoopers en uitgevers in Noord-Nederland sedert de uitvinding van de boekdrukkunst tot den aanvang der negentiende eeuw. Eene proeve. *Deventer,* 1872, 4to *Not printed for sale*

LEDEBOER (A. M.). Het geslacht van Waesberghe. Eene bijdrage tot de geschiedenis der Boekdrukkunst en van den Boekhandel in Nederland. *s' Gravenhage,* 1869, 8vo

LEE (A. van). Haarlem's regt op de eer van de uitvinding der Boekdrukkunst gehandhaafd; of beknopt overzigt van den Stand der Zaak, vooral na het onderzoek van den Heer de Vries, en de toelichtingen van de Heeren Schinkel en Noordziek. *Amsterdam,* 1813, 8vo *Not printed for sale*

LEFÈVRE (Théotiste). Guide pratique du compositeur d'imprimerie. *Paris,* 1855, 8vo

LEFÈVRE (T.). Instruction pour la Composition du Grec, extrait d'un ouvrage inédit intitulé, "Le Guide du Compositeur." *Paris,* 1847, 8º

LEFÈVRE (T.). Nouvelle classification de la Casse Française. *St. Germain,* 1833, 4º

LEFÈVRE (T.). Recueil d'Impositions exécutées en Caractères mobiles, suivi d'une nouvelle Classification de la Casse Française. *Paris,* 1838 and 1848, *oblong* 8º

LEGOUVÉ (Ernest). La Découverte de l'Imprimerie. Pièce en vers qui a remporté le prix de Poésie décerné par l'Académie Française, 1829. *Paris,* 1829, 8º

LEHNE (Friedrich). Einige Bemerkungen über das unternehmen der gelehrten Gesellschaft zu Harlem, ihrer Stadt die Ehre der Erfindung der Buchdruckerkunst zu ertrotzen; nebst einem nachtrage, veranlasst durch eine sogenannte Recension in der Hallischen Litteraturzeitung. *Mainz*, 1823, 8*vo*

LEHNE (F.). Historisch-critische prüfung der Ansprüche, welche die Stadt Haarlem auf den Ruhm der Erfindung der Buchdruckerkunst macht, durch Beleuchtung der Ansichten ihrer Vertheidiger: des Heern Dr. Ebert, Hofbibliothekars zu Dresden, und des Herrn Koning, Obergerichtschreibers zu Amsterdam. *Mainz*, 1827, 8*vo*

LEICH (John Henry). De Origine et Incrementis Typographiæ Lipsiensis liber singularis, ubi varia de Literariis urbis studiis et viris doctis, qui in ea claruerunt, inserunter. Accedit Librorum Sec. XV. Excusorum ad Maittairii Annales Supplementum. *Lipsiæ* [1740], 4*to*

LEIPZIG. Programm der vierten Säcularfeier der Erfindung der Buchdruckerkunst. Leipzig, den 24., 25. und 26. Juni, 1840, 4*to*

LEIPZIG. Verzeichniss der Gegenstände welche zur vierten Säcularfeier der Buchdruckerkunst in der Deutschen Buchhändlerbörse in Leipzig ausgestellt sind. *Leipzig*, 1840, 8*vo*

LEMOINE (Henry). Typographical Antiquities. History, Origin, and Progress of the Art of Printing, from its first invention in Germany to the end of the seventeenth century, and from its Introduction into England, by Caxton, to the present time, including, among a variety of curious and interesting matter, its progress in the Provinces, with chronological Lists of Eminent Printers in England, Scotland, and Ireland, a curious Dissertation on the Origin of the use of Paper, also a complete history of the art of wood-cutting and engraving on copper, from its first invention in Italy to its latest improvement in Great Britain . . extracted from the best authorities. *London*, 1797, *small* 8*vo*

LEMOINE (H.). Typographical Antiquities. 2nd edition, corrected and enlarged by T. A., of the Inner Temple, Esq. *London*, 1813, *sm.* 8*vo*

LEMPERTZ (Heinrich). Beiträge zur altern Geschichte der Buchdruck und Holzschneidekunst. Erster heft. *Koln*, 1839, 4*to*

LEMPERTZ (H.). Bibliographische und Xylographische Versuche. Erster heft (*all published*). *Koln*, 1838, 4*to* *Only 30 copies printed for private circulation*

LEMPERTZ (H.). Bilder-Hefte zur Geschichte des Bücherhandels und der mit demselben verwandten Künste und Gewerbe. *Cöln*, 1853-65, *folio*

LEMPERTZ (H.). Insignien berühmter Druckereien der 15. Jahrhundert, welche bei Rothscholz fehlen. *Köln*, 1839, *4to*

LENNEP (G. van). Beschrijving van het Handschrift der Batavia van H. Junius. *'s Gravenhage*, 1840, *8vo*

LENNEP (G. van). Bijdrage tot de Geschiedenis van de Uitvinding der Boekdrukkunst. 1809, *8vo*

LENNEP (G. van). Wederlegging van het Geschrift van den Heere J. Koning over de Aanmerkingen wegens den houten Druk-vorm. *8vo*

LESSEL (J. C.). Die edle Buchdrucker-Kunst als ein von Gott gesch. Hülffs-Mittel z. Fortpflantz. d. Glaubens. *Brieg*, 1740, 4º

LESSER (Friedrich Christian). Typographia Jubilans. Das ist: Kurtzgefaszte Historie der Buchdruckerey, worinnen von dieser edlen Kunst Ursprunge und Anfange, Ausbreitung, Verbesserung, Zierrathen, Nutzen, Wie nicht weniger von der Buchdrucker Eigenschafften und Pflichten, und dann von anderer Verhalten gegen dieselbe und deren Kunst-Verwandten kürtzlich gehandeltwird. *Leipzig*, 1740, *8vo*

LETTRE d'un Amatur au Rédacteur du Mercure au sujet des Nouveaux Caractères de M. Didot. *Paris*, 8º

LEVEZOW (J. F.). Die Wanderung der Buchdruckerkunst, etc. *Stettin*, 1777-9, 4º

LEVOL (Florimond). L'Invention de l'imprimerie. Poëme. *Paris*, 1829, *8vo*

LEVRAY (Alphonse). Gutenberg, Scènes historiques. *Paris*, 1856, 8º [*Reprinted from L'Ami de la Jeunesse, Nos. 3, 4, and 5, 1856*]

LEWIS (J.). Life of W. Caxton. *London*, 1737, *royal 8vo Portrait*

LICHTENBERGER (Johann Friedrich). Geschichte der Erfindung der Buchdruckerkunst zur Ehrenrettung Strassburgs, und vollständiger Widerlegung der Sagen von Harlem. Mit einem Vorberichte von J. G. Schweighäuser. *Strassburg*, 1825, *8vo*

LICHTENBERGER (J. F.). Histoire de l'Invention de l'Imprimerie, pour servir de défense à la Ville de

Strasbourg contre les prétentions de Harlem. **Avec une** Préface de M. J. G. Schweighæuser. *Strasbourg*, 1825, 8vo

LICHTENBERGER (J. F.). Initia Typographica illustravit. *Argentorati*, 1811, 4to

LICHTENBERGER (J. F.). Indulgentiarum Literas Nicolai V. P. M. pro regno Cypri impressus **anno** 1454 matricumque epocham vindicavit Initia Typographica supplevit. *Argentorati*, 1816, 4º

LINDE (A. van der). De Haarlemsche **Costerlegende**. *s'Gravenhage*, 1870, 8vo

LINDE (A. van der). The **Haarlem Legend of the** Invention of **Printing by** Lourens Janszoon Coster. From **the Dutch by** J. H. Hessels, with an Introduction **and a** classified list of the **Costerian** Incunabula. *London*, 1871, 8vo

LION (A.). **Ueber Bücher-Correctur.** *Göttingen*, 1852, 8º

LION (I. J.). Stenographie en Tachygraphie. *s'Gravenhage*, 1849, 8vo

LISCH (G. C. F.). Geschichte der Buchdruckerkunst in Mecklenburg bis **zur jahr 1540.** *Schwerin*, 1839, 8vo

LITHOGRAPHIE: Organ für Lithographie und verwandte **Fächer.** *Hamburg*, 1861-2, 4º

LITHOGRAPHY. Algemeene Ophelderende Verklaring van het Oud Letterschrift, in Steenplaatdruk. *Leyden*, 1818, 12mo **text** and 4to *Atlas*

LITHOGRAPHY. Le Petit Manuel du Lithographe. *Paris*, 1832, 4to

LIVY. Romische **Historie** uss Tito Livio gezogen. *Mentz*, J. *Schöffer*, 1505, *folio* [*Printed by* **the son** *of Peter Schöffer. The title-page,* **which** *is nearly always wanting,* **has on its reverse** *a preface* **which** *concludes with* **a** *statement* **of the** *invention of* print*ing by* **Gutenburg in** *Mentz* **1450***, and that* **he was** *aided by* **Johan Faust and Peter** *Schöffer*]

LOGOTETA (I.). Spicilegium Typographicum de Siculis editionibus sæculi XV. *Palermo*, 1807, 8º

LOMBARDI (Andrea). Sulle vicende della tipografia Cosentina. *Cosenza*, 1816, 8º

LONDON Scale of Prices for Compositors' Work, agreed upon April 16, 1810. *London*, n. d. 12mo

LONGHI (Giuseppe). La Calcografia propriamente detta, ossia l'Arte d'Incidere in rame coll' acquaforte, col bulino e colla punta. Vol. I. Concernante la Teorica dell' Arte. *Milano*, 1833, 8*vo* [*all published*]

Loosjes (A.). Laurens Koster, tooneelstuk. 1808, 8º

Loosjes (Vincent). Gedenkschriften wegens het vierde eeuwgetijde van de uitvinding der boekdrukkunst door Laurens Janszoon Coster, van Stadswege gevierd te Haarlem den 10 en 11 Julij, 1823. *Haarlem*, 1824, 8*vo*

Loots (Cornelis). Feestzang bij de viering van het vierde eeuwfeest der uitvinding van de Boekdrukkunst, te Haarlem. *Amsterdam*, 1823, 8*vo*

Lorck (C. B.). Die Herstellung von Druckwerken. *Leipzig*, 1869, 8*vo*

Lottin (A. M.). Catalogue Chronologique des Libraires et Libraires Imprimeurs de Paris depuis l'an 1470. 2 vols. *Paris*, 1789, 8º

Loyson et Briquet. Epreuve des Caractères de la Fonderie de. *Paris*, 1751, 4º

Luce (L.). Essai d'une nouvelle Typographie ornée de vignettes, fleurons, trophées, filets, cadres et cartels, inventés, dessinés, et executés par L. Luce, graveur du roi, pour son Imprimerie Royale. *Paris, Barbou*, 1771, 4*to*

Luckombe (P.). The History and Art of Printing in two parts [*here follows contents*]. The whole forming a more intelligible and complete introduction to the Art of Printing than has been hitherto attempted, and containing a great variety of Instructions and Examples that are not to be found in any other Performance. *London*, 1771, 8*vo*

Lunze (Jo. Gott.). Monumentorum Typographicorum, Decas. *Lipsiæ*, 1799, 12º

Lynch (Thos.). The Printer's Manual; a Practical Guide for Compositors and Pressmen. *Cincinnati*, 1859, 16*mo*

Lyons. Manuel de Bibliophile et de l'Archéologie Lyonnais. *Paris*, 1857, 8*vo*

McCorquodale and Co's Specimens of Book Work. *London*, 1849, 4to

Macintosh (C. A.). Popular Outlines of the Press, Ancient and Modern. *London*, n. d. 12mo

Mackeller (Thos.). The American Printer. A manual of Typography; containing complete instruction for Beginners, as well as Practical Directions for Managing every Department of a Printing Office. With several useful Tables, schemes for imposing forms in every variety, hints to Authors and Publishers, &c. *Philadelphia*, 1866, 12mo

MacCreery (John). The Press a Poem. 2 parts. *Liverpool*, 1803-27, 4to

MacCreery (J.). The Press, A Poem, in two parts. With other Pieces. Second edition. *London*, 1828, 8°

Madden (J. P. A.). Lettres d'un Bibliographe, *four series*. *Paris*, 1868-1875, 8vo

Madinier (Henry). Exposition Universelle de 1855. Notes sur les principaux Produits exposés de l'Imprimerie. *Paris*, 1855, 8°

Madinier (Henry) et Parrot (A.). Amour et Typographie. Comédie-Vaudeville en deux actes. *Paris*, 1856, 8vo *One of the two copies printed on "papier d'Hollande"*

Maffei (G.). Storia della Letteratura Italiana dall' origine della lingua fino al secolo XIX. 5 vols. *Napoli*, 1829, 12°

Magasin Typographique. *Basle*, 1864-5, 8°

Mahncke (G. H.). Johannes von Guttenberg und Dr. Joh. Faust. Dramat. Erzählt. *Hamburg*, 1809, sm. 8°

Maimieux (J. de). Pasigraphie ... nouvel art-science d'écrire et d'imprimer en une langue à manière d'être lu et entendu dans toute autre langue. *Paris*, 1797, 4to

Mairet (F.). Notice sur la Lithographie, deuxième

édition, suivie d'un Essai sur la Reliure et le blanchiment des Livres et Gravures. *Châtillon sur Seine*, 1824, 12mo *5 plates*

MAITTAIRE (Michael). Annales Typographici ab Artis inventæ Origine ad Annum 1500. *Hagæ Comitum*, 1719—vol. ii. 1500-1536, *Hagæ Comitum*, 1722—vol. iii. 1536-1557, *Hagæ Comitum*, 1722—vol. iv. [*a new edition of vol.* i.] *Amstelodami*, 1733—vol. v. Index, *Londini*, 1741. Together, 5 vols. in nine parts, 4to Supplement by Denis, 2 vols. 1789, 4to

MAITTAIRE (M.). Annales Typographici, &c. 9 vols. *Hag. Com.* 1719-41, 4to *Large paper*

MAITTAIRE (M.). Historia Typographorum aliquot Parisiensium vitas et libros complectens. 2 vols. *Londini*, 1717, 8vo

MAITTAIRE (M.). Stephanorum Historia, Vitas ipsorum ac libros complectens. 2 vols. in 1. *Londini*, 1709, 8vo *Portrait of Robert Stephens*

MALDOW (A.). Die Buchdruckerkunst, &c. *Leipzig*, 1871, 4°

MALLINKROT (Bernard). De Ortu ac Progressu Artis Typographicæ, Dissertatio Historica in qua Præter alia pleraque ad Calcographices Negocium Spectantia de Auctoribus et Loco inventionis præcipuè inquiritur, proque Moguntinis contra Harlemenses concluditur. *Coloniæ Agrippinæ*, 1640, 4to *Engraved title containing portrait of author*

MAME. Ad. Mame et Cie. à Tours. Imprimerie-Librairie-Reliure. Notice et Documents. *Tours*, 1862, 4to *Plates by Gustave Doré and others*

MANNI (Domenico Maria). Vita di Aldo Pio Manuzio, insigne restauratore delle lettere greche e latine in Venezia. *Venezia*, 1759, 8vo *Portrait of Aldus engraved by Baratti*

MANNI (D. M.). Vita di Pietro Perna, Lucchese, diligentissimo Impressore in Basilia. *Lucca*, 1763, 8vo

MANUEL (Le) des Impositions Typographiques, suivi d'une planche où l'on trouve la manière de corriger les épreuves d'Imprimerie et de la représentation de la Casse Romaine et Grecque Simple. Seconde édition augmentée. *Paris*, 1792, 8°

MANUZIO (Paolo). Lettere, copiate sugli autografi esistenti nella Biblioteca Ambrosiana. *Parigi*, 1834, 8°

MANZONI (G.). Annali Tipografici **Torinese** del secolo XV. *Torino*, 1863, 8º

MARAHENS (August). Vollständig theoretisch-praktisches Handbuch der Typographie nach ihrem heutigen **Standpunkte. 2** vols. *Leipzig*, 1870, *8vo*

MARAHENS (A.). Haandbog i Bogtrykkerkunsten, tildeels udarbeidet efter fremmede kilder, navnlig Aug. Marahens "Handbuch der Typographie, nach ihrem **heutigen Standpunkte.**" *Kjobenhavn*, 1872, 8º

MARCEL (M. J. J.). Alphabet Arabe, Turc, et Parsan, à l'usage de l'Imprimerie Orientale et Française. *Alexandrie*, 1796, 4º

MARCHAND (Prosper). Histoire de l'Origine et des premiers Progrès de l'Imprimerie. *La Haye*, 1740, 4to.—Supplement [*by the Abbé St. Léger*]. *Paris*, 1773, *4to*

MARCHAND. Supplément à l'Histoire de l'Imprimerie de Prosper Marchand: ou additions et corrections pour cet ouvrage. Edition revue et augmentée: avec un Mémoire sur l'Epoque certaine du Commencement de l'année à Mayence durant le XVᵉ Siècle. *Paris*, 1775, 4to

MARINONI. "The Echo" Marinoni Printing Machine, at the International Exhibition, London, 1872. **24º**

MARLOW (F.). Gutenberg. Drama in fünf Aufzügen. *Leipzig*, 1840, *8vo*

MARNIX (C. H. R.). Mentz of Haarlem? Johann Genfleisch von Gutenberg of Laurens Janszoon Koster? eene Bijdrage tot de Geschiedenis van de uitvinding der Boekdrukkunst. *'s Gravenhage*, 1852, *8vo*

MAROCCO (Maurizio). Cenni sull' origine e sui progressi dell' arte tipografica in Torino dal 1474 al 1861. *Torino*, 1861, 12mo

MAROLLES (Magné de). Recherches sur l'Origine et le premier usage des registres, des signatures, des réclaimes, et des chiffres de page dans les livres imprimés. *Paris*, 1782, 12º

MAROUZE (P. H. de). Histoire de l'Imprimerie. *Paris*, 1862, 8º

MARR, GALLIE and Co. Specimen of Types. *London*, 1843, *oblong* 4to

MARTIAL (A. P.). Nouveau Traité de la Gravure à l'eau forte. *Paris*, 1873, *8vo*

MARTIN (B.). Typographia Naturalis: or the Art of Printing, or taking impressions from Natural Subjects. *London*, 1772, 8*vo*

MARTIN (M.). Les Origines de l'Alphabet. *Paris*, 1859, 8*vo*

MASON (William). The Printer's Assistant, containing a sketch of the history of printing, an Essay on Punctuation, various Typographical Tables, &c. Fourth edition. *London* [1823], 8º

MASSEY (W.). Origin and Progress of Letters. *London*, 1763, 8*vo*

MASSMAN (H. F.). Die Xylographa der Kon. Hof und Staats Bibliothek sowie der Kon. Univ. bibliothek in München. *Leipzig*, 1841, 8*vo*

MASSON (Georges). Les Arts graphiques à l'Exposition de Vienne (groupe XII): imprimerie et librairie, lithographie, gravure en taille-douce, sur bois, etc. *Paris*, 1875, 8º

MAYENCE. Gedenk-buch der IV$_n$ Jubelfeier der Erfindung der Buchdruckerkunst in Mainz. *Mainz*, 1840, *royal* 8*vo* *Plates*

MAZZUCOTELLI (Ant.). L'arte del Guttemberg, ossia la Stampa. *Torino*, 1863, 8º

MEERMAN (Gerard). Conspectus Originum Typographicarum, proxime in lucem edendarum. 1761, *sm.* 8*vo*

MEERMAN (G.). Plan du Traité des Origines Typographiques. Traduit du Latin en François [par l'abbé Goujet]. *Paris*, 1762, *sm.* 8*vo*

MEERMAN (G.). Origines Typographicæ. 2 vols. *Hagæ Comitum*, 1765, 4*to* *Plates*

MEERMAN. *Another copy on large and fine paper, the author's copy*

MEERMAN (G.). De l'Invention de l'Imprimerie ou Analyse des deux ouvrages publiés sur cette matière par M. Meerman. Suivi d'une notice chronologique et raisonnée des livres avec et sans date imprimés avant l'année 1501 dans les dix-sept Provinces des Pays Bas par M. Jaques Visser; et augmentée d'environ deux cents articles par l'éditeur [Jansen]. *Paris*, 1809, 8*vo*

MEERMAN (G.). Uitvinding der boekdrukkunst, en aanteekeningen van Henrik Gockinga, getrokken uit het latynsch werk van Gerard Meerman met eene voorreden hierachter is gevoegt ene lyst der Boeken in de Nederlanden gedrukt voor't jaar MD. opgestelt door **Jakob** Visser. *Amsteldam,* 1767, **4to**

MEERMAN. *Another copy with a large number of annotations and corrections in Visser's list by C. G. Hultman*

MEERSCH (P. C. van der). Gérard Leeu, imprimeur à Gouda et à **Anvers,** de 1477-93. **2 parts.** *Gand,* c. 1845, 8º

MEERSCH (P. C. **van der).** Recherches sur **la vie et les** travaux de quelques Imprimeurs Belges pendant les XV et XVI siècles. 3 parts. *Gand,* 1844, 8vo

MEERSCH (P. C. van der). Recherches **sur la vie et les travaux** des imprimeurs Belges et Néerlandais **établis à** l'étranger, et sur la part qu'ils ont prise à la régénération littéraire de l'Europe au XVe Siècle, précédées d'une **Introduction** Historique sur la Découverte de l'Imprimerie et sur la Propagation de cet Art en Belgique et en Hollande. Vol. i. **(all** published). *Gand,* 1856, 8vo

MEERSCH (P. C. van der). Un mot sur la Question de l'Invention de l'Imprimerie, à propos de l'Essai Historique et Critique sur l'Invention de l'Imprimerie par M. Ch. Paeille. *Gand,* 1860, 8vo

MEGERLINUS (D. F.). **Annus** Bibliorum, 1450, primo impressorum **Moguntiæ,** Tertium Jubilaris, hoc anno 1750. *Francofurti,* 1750, *sm.* **4to**

MELE (Carlo). Degli **odierni ufficî** della Tipografia e dei libri; discorso pratico ed economico. *Napoli,* 1834, 16º

MENDEZ (Francisco). Typographia Española, ò **Historia** de **la** introduccion, propagacion, **y** progresos del **Arte** de la Imprenta en España. A la que antecede **una** Noticia general sobre la Imprenta de la Europa, y de la China, adornado todo con **Notas** instructivas **y** curiosas. Tomo i. *Madrid,* 1796, *sm.* **4to** [*All published, the MS. of vol.* i. *having been lost*]

MENDEZ (F.). Tipografia Española . . . Segunda Edicion corregida y adicionada por Don Dionisio Hidalgo. *Madrid,* 1861, *royal 8vo*

MENTEL (Jacob). Excursus de Loco et Auctore Inventionis Typographicæ. *Paris,* 1644, 4º

MENTEL (J.). De vera Typographiæ Origine paraenesis. *Paris,* 1650, 4to

MERLIN (B.). Origine des cartes à jouer, recherches nouvelles sur les Naïbis, les Tarots et sur les autres espèces de cartes. *Paris*, 1869, 4to *73 plates*

MÉRY et de NERVAL. L'Imagier de Harlem, ou la découverte de l'Imprimerie, Drame-Légende. *Paris*, 1851, 8vo

METZ (FRIEDERICH). Geschichte des Buchhandels und der Buchdruckerkunst. *Darmstadt*,1834-35,8vo

MEURS (P. van). De Keulsche Kronick en de Costerlegende van Dr. A. Van der Linde te zamen getoetst. *Haarlem*, 1870, 8vo

MEUSCHEN (J. G.). Der... Rechte Abdruck der Person Christi... Als der auch hie in Coburg celebr. Jubel-Feyer der Buchdruckerey. *Coburg*, 1740, 8°

MEYER (Heinrich). Addressbuch der Buchdruckereien von Mitteleuropa. *Braunschweig*, 1854, 8°

MEYER (H.). Gutenbergs-Album. *Braunschweig*, 1840, 4to

MEYER (H.). Handbuch der Stereotypie. *Braunschweig*, 1838, 8°

MEYER (L. E.). Die Buchdruckerkunst in Augsburg. *Augsburg*, 1840, royal 8vo

MEZGER (G. C.). Augsburg älteste Druckdenkmale und Formschneiderarbeiten. *Augsburg*, 1840, roy. 8vo

MICHELETTI (G. B.). Presagi scientifici sull' arte della Stampa. *Aquila*, 1814, 8°

MIDDLETON (Conyers). A Dissertation concerning the Origin of Printing in England. Shewing that it was first introduced and practised by our Countryman, William Caxton, at Westminster: and not, as is commonly believed, by a Foreign Printer at Oxford. *Cambridge*, 1735, 4to

MIDDLETON (C.). Dissertation sur l'Origine de l'Imprimerie en Angleterre, traduite de l'Anglaise par D. G. Imbert. *Paris*, 1775, 8vo

MILAN. Statuti et Ordini della Università de Librari et Stampatori della città di Milano. *Milano*, 1614, 4°

MILAN. Statuto del Circolo Italiano della Libreria, Tipografia ed arti affini. *Milano*, 1863, 8vo

MILLER and Co. (William). Specimen of Printing Types. *Edinburgh*, 1813, 4to

MILLER and RICHARD. Specimen of Book and Magazine Founts. *Edinburgh and London, no date*, 4to

MINZLOFF (Charles R.). Souvenir de la Bibliothèque Imperiale **Publique de St. Petersbourg.** *Leipzig*, 1863, **4to**

MIOZZO (Gaetano). Cenni biografici su G. B. Bodoni. *Torino*, 1872, 8º

MIRA (Guiseppe M.). A quale città di Sicilia spetta il primato della introduzione della Stampa, lettera. *Palermo*, 1874, 12mo

MIRA (G. M.). Manuale teorico-pratico **di bibliografia. 2 vols.** *Palermo*, 1863, 8º

MIRA (G. M.). Sull' introduzione dell' arte tipo**grafica in Palermo,** riflessioni. *Palermo*, 1859, 8º

MIRROR of TYPOGRAPHY (The). T. H. Senior & Co. Monthly. *New York*, 1869, 4to

MITCHEL's **Type** Setting **by** Machinery, **with Opin**ions of the **Press,** etc. *London*, 1863, 8vo

MOHNIKE (Gottlieb). Die Geschichte **der Buch**druckerkunst in Pommern. *Stettin*, 1840, 8vo

MOHNIKE (G.). Geschichte der Buchdruckereien in Stralsund bis 1809. *Stralsund*, 1833, 4to

MOLE JEUNE. Collection typographique, &c. *Paris (Didot)*, 1819, 8º

MOLHUYSEN (P. C.). Procedure over de werken van David Joris. [*Arnheim*, 1850], 8vo

MOLLER (Daniel. Giul.). Dissertatio de Typographià. *Altorfi*, **1692**, 4to *5 portraits*

MOMMAAS (C.). Laurens Coster. Tijdschrift voor Beoefenaren en **voorstanders** der Boekdrukkunst. *Utrecht*, 1859, **12mo**

MOMMAAS (C.). Lettergieterij, **Boek-en Plaatdrukkerij.** *Amsterdam*, 1860, 8vo

MOMORO (Ant. Franc.). Traité Elémentaire de l'Imprimerie ou le Manuel l'Imprimeur. *Paris*, 1796, 8vo

MOMORO (A. F.). Le Manuel des Impositions Typographiques, où l'on trouve aussi la représentation de la **Casse Romaine,** Grecque simple, Anglaise et Ronde, ainsi que la Manière de composer l'Anglaise et celle de corriger les Epreuves d'Imprimerie. Extrait du grand ouvrage de M. Momoro. *Bruxelles*, 1819, 8º

Monet (A. L.). Le Conducteur de Machines Typographiques, Guide Practique, Etudes sur les différents systèmes de machines mise en train-découpages. *Paris*, 1872, 12*mo*

Monumenta Typographica, quæ exstant in bibliotheca Collegii Canonicorum Regularium in Rebdorf, collegit, notis illustravit et edidit ejusdem Collegii Bibliothecarius A.D. 1787. *Eichstadii* [1787], 4*to*

Morelli (Jacopo). Aldi Pii Manutii scripta tria longe rarissima a Jacobo Morellio denuo edita et illustrata. *Bassani*, 1806, 16°

Morelli (J.). Essais sur l'histoire de l'Imprimerie à Venise. 3 vols. *Venezia*, 1820, 8°

Morelli (J.). Monumenti del principio della Stampa in Venezia. *Venezia*, 1793, 4°

Moreni (D.). Annali della Tipografia Fiorentina di Lorenzo Torrentino, 1547-63. *Firenze*, 1819, 8*vo*

Mores (Edward Rowe). A Dissertation upon English Typographic Founders and Founderies (with Appendix by J. Nichols). [*London*], 1778, 8*vo Only Eighty copies printed*

Mortimer (Cromwell). Account of the principles of Christopher de Blon of Printing in Imitation of Painting. [*Philosophical Transactions Abridged*, vol. vii. p. 477], 1731, 4°

Mortimer (C.). Of an Antique Metal Stamp. [*Phil. Trans. Abr.*] 1738, 4°

Morton (George H.). The History of Paper Hangings with a Review of other modes of Mural Decoration. *Liverpool*, 1875, 8°

Motteley (Charles). Aperçu sur les Erreurs de la Bibliographie Spéciale des Elzévirs et de leurs annexes, avec quelques découvertes curieuses sur la Typographie Hollandaise et Belge du XVIIe Siècle; par le Bibliophile Ch. M. *Paris*, 1847, 12*mo 240 copies printed*

Motteley (C.). Essai Bibliographique sur les éditions des Elzévirs. *Paris*, 1822, 8*vo*

Motteroz. Essai sur les Gravures Chimiques en relief. *Paris*, 1871, 8*vo*

Moulinet (J. E. V.). Album du Typographe. Livr. 1 and 2 [Guttenberg and Beranger]. *Paris*, 1858, 4*to*

Moxon (Joseph). Mechanick Exercises. 2 vols. [*The second volume*, 1683, *is entirely " applied to the Art of Printing."*] London, 1677-83, 4to

Moxon (J.). Rules of the Three Orders of Print Letters, viz. the Roman, Italic, and English Capitals and Small. *London*, 1676, 4to *Plates*

Moyes (J.). Specimens of the Types commonly used in the Temple Printing Office, Bouverie Street. *London*, 1826, 8vo

Mueller (F.). Iets over den Letterkundigen Eigendom. *'s Gravenhage*, 1852, 12mo

Mueller (Joseph). Ein Autographon Peter Schoeffer's in einer incunabel der Koeniglichen und Universitaets-Bibliothek zu Koenigsberg I. Pr. mit lithographirtem facsimile. *Koenigsberg I. Pr.*, 1869, 4°

Mueller (J. I.). Die Leipziger Buchdruckeren nach ihrer ersten Beschaffenheit. *Leipzig* [1720], 4°

Mueller (N.). Beschreibung des Festes dem andenken des Erfinders der Buchdruckerkunst Johann Gensfleisch zum Gutenberg, gefeiert in Mainz am 4. Oktober 1824, von sämmtlichen Herren Schriftsetzern, Buchdruckern und Schriftgiessern daselbst, bei Gelegenheit der Einweihung des dem grossen Erfinder von der Casino-Gesellschaft im Hofe zum Gutenberg gesetzten Denksteins. *Mainz*, 1824, 8vo

Munch-Schaubert-Negelein. Primaria quædam Documenta de Origine Typographiæ. Quorum illustratorum partem primam sub præsidio Christiani Gottlibii Schwarzii . . . a. d. xii. Novembris A. S. R. MDCCXXXX Disquisitione Academicæ subiicit Benedictus Guilielmus Munch. *Altorfii* [1740], 4to

    Partem Alteram . . . ad Disquirendum proponit Io. Guilielmus Schaubert. *Altorfii* [1740], 4to

    Partem Tertiam . . . Disputandi Caussa proponit Gustavus Philippus Negelein. *Altorfii* [1740], 4to

Munden (Christian). Danck Predigt welche am dritten Jubelfest wegen erfindung der Löbl. Buchdruckerkunst. *Franckfurt*, 1741, 12mo

Munier (J. B.). Almanach-Guide de l'Imprimerie, de la Librairie et de la Papeterie. Indispensable aux Auteurs, Editeurs, Libraires, Ouvriers d'Imprimerie, Brocheurs, Relieurs, &c. Indiquant la division, le poids, la qualité, le format des papiers, la composition des volumes et les signes de correction. *Paris*, 1870, 8°

Muzzi (Salvatore). La Stampa in Bologna: sommario storico. *Bologna*, 1869, 4°

ACHRICHTEN (Neueste), von der Schreib-und Druckfreyheit in Schweden. *Stralsund*, 1778, 8°

Nagler (G. K.). Alois Senefelder und der geistliche Rath Simon Schmid als Rivalen in der Geschichte der Erfindung des mechanischen Steindruckes, nicht der Lithographie in höherer Bedeutung. *München*, 1862, 8vo

Nagler (G. K.). Neues allgemeines Künstler-Lexikon, oder Nachrichten von dem Leben und den Werken der Maler, Bildhauer, Baumeister, Kupferstecher, Formschneider, Lithographen, Zeichner, Medailleure, Elfenbeinarbeiter, etc. 22 vols. *Munchen*, 1835-52, 8°

Napione (Gianfrancesco Galeani). Osservazione intorno alle ricerche riguardanti l'origine della Stampe della figure in legno ed in rame. 1806, 4to

Nast (Johannes). Historisch-Critische-Nachrichten von den sechs ersten Teutschen Bibel-Ausgaben, die zu Maynz, Strasburg und Augspurg vom 1462, bis zum Jahr 1477 find gedrukt worden; aus der Herzoglich-Württembergischen Consistorial-Bibliothek zu Stuttgard, und aus schriftlichen Beyträgen, nebst einer Critischen Anzeige aller übrigen vor Luthero theils wirklichen theils vermeintlichen Bibel-Ausgaben. *Stuttgard*, 1767, 12°

Natolini (G. B.). Discorso intorno l'arte della Stampa. *Udine*, 1606, f°

Née de la Rochelle (J. F.). Eloge Historique de Jean Gensfleisch dit Guttenberg, premier inventeur de l'Art Typographique à Mayence. *Paris*, 1811, 8vo

Née de la Rochelle (J. F.). Recherches historiques et critiques sur l'Etablissement de l'Art Typographique en Espagne et en Portugal. *Paris*, 1830, *8vo*

Née de la Rochelle (J. F.). Vie d'Etienne Dolet, imprimeur à Lyon dans le seizième siècle, avec une notice des libraires et imprimeurs auteurs que l'on a pu découvrir jusqu'à ce jour. *Paris*, 1779, *8vo*

Neuburger (H.). Encyklopädie der Buchdruckerkunst. *Leipzig*, 1844, 8º

Neuburger (H.). Praktisches Handbuch der Buchdruckerkunst. *Dessau*, 1840, 8º

Nichols (John). Biographical and Literary Anecdotes of William Bowyer, Printer. *London*, 1782, 4to

Nichols (J.). Biographical Memoirs of William Ged; including a particular account of his Progress in the art of Block-Printing *London*, 1781, 8º; *Newcastle*, 1819, 8º

Nierstrasz (J. L.). Eeuwzang bij het vierde Eeuwgetijde van de uitvinding der Boekdrukkunst. 1840, *8vo*

Niesert (J.). Beiträge zur Buchdruckergeschichte Munsters. *Coesfeld*, 1828, *8vo*

Niesert (J.). Beweis der Originalität der von J. Mentelin vor 1466 gedruckten. *Coesfeld*, 1825, *8vo*

Niesert (J.). Literärische Nachricht über die erste zu Köln gedruckte Nieder-Deutsche Bibel. *Coesfeld*, 1825, *8vo*

Nisard (Charles). Histoire des Livres Populaires. 2 vols. *Paris*, 1854, *8vo Large Paper*

Nodier (C.). Des Annales de l'Imprimerie des Aldes. *Paris*, 1835, 8º

Noordziek (J. J. F.). Beschrijving van twee prachtexemplaren der in het Fransch uitgegeven werken van der Heer A. de Vries, over de Uitvinding der Boekdrukkunst [1846], 8º *Not published for sale*

Noordziek (J. J. F.). Gedenkboek der Costers-Feesten van 15, 16 en 17 Julij, 1856. *Harlem*, 1858, *8vo*

Noordziek (J. J. F.). Het geschilstuk betrekkelijk de uitvinding der Boekdrukkunst. *Harlem*, 1848, *8vo*

NOORDZIEK (J. J. F.). Levensschets van A. D. Schinkel. *Leiden*, 1865, 8vo

NORDISK Boktryckeri-Tidning. Monthly. *Stockholm, January*, 1870, 4to *In Progress*

NOTES sur G. Silvius imprimeur d'Anvers, 1560-79. *Bruxelles*, 1862, 8º

NOTICE sur la Fonte des Types mobiles d'un Caractère Chinois, gravé sur acier par Marcellin Legrand. *Paris*, 1836, 8º

NOUVEAU procédé typographique, qui réunit les avantages de l'imprimerie mobile et du stéréotypage. *Paris*, 1822, 8º

NUYTS (C. J.). Essai sur l'imprimerie des Nutius. *Bruxelles*, 1856, 8vo *Only fifty copies printed*

NYENHUIS (J. T. Bodel). De juribus typographorum et bibliopolarum in regno Belgico. *Lugd. Bat.* 1819, 8vo *Large paper in 4to*

NYENHUIS (J. T. Bodel). Dissertatione historico juridico de juribus typographorum et bibliopolarum in Regno Neerl. *Lugd. Bat.* 1819, 8vo *Large paper in 4to*

NYENHUIS (J. T. Bodel). Liste alphabétique d'une collection de portraits d'imprimeurs, de libraires etc. 6 parts. *Leide*, 1836-68, 4to

NYROP (Camillus). Bidrag til den Danske Bokhandels Historie. Trykt som Manuscript. Til minde om den Gyldendalske Boghandels hundredaarige Jubiläum. *Köbenhavn*, 1870, 8vo

BERLIN (Jer. Jacques). Essai d'Annales de la Vie de Jean Guttenberg, Inventeur de la Typographie. *Strasbourg*, 1801, 8vo *Portrait of Gutenberg*

OELRICHS (J. C. C.). Nachricht von der Vortrefflichen ehemaligen fürstl. Buchdruckerey zu Bard in Pommern. *Butzow*, 1756, 8º

OLDYS (Wm.). The British Librarian: exhibiting a compendious Review or Abstract of our most scarce, useful and valuable Books in all sciences as well in Manuscript as in Print. *London*, 1738, 8vo

OLEARIUS (J. C.). Löbl. Buchdruckerkunst. *Halle* [1640], *small 4to*

OLIVEIRA (José de). Diagnosis Typografica dos Caracteres Gregos, Hebraicos e Arabigos, addicionada com algumas notes sobre a divisão orthografica da lingua Latina, e outras da Europa, a que se ajuntão alguns preceitos da Arte Typografica para melhor correção, e uso dos Compositores e Apprendizes da Imprensa Regia. *Lisboa*, 1804, 8º

OOMKENS (J.). Bouwstoffen toteene geschiedenis van de boekdrukkunst en den boekhandel in de stad en provincie Groningen. [*Groningen*], 1854, 8vo *Not printed for sale*

OPITIUS (J. C.). Incunabula atque Incrementa Typographiæ sæculo XV. *Mindæ*, 1740, 4º

OPITIUS (J. C.). Singularia artis Typographiæ a Sæculo XVI. Schediasmata III. *Mindæ*, 1743, 4º

ORATIO DOMINICA. CL linguis versa, edente denuò J. J. Marcel. *Paris*, 1818, 4to

ORLANDI (Pellegrini Antonio). Origine e Progressi della Stampa o sia dell' Arte Impressoria e Notizie dell' Opere Stampate, dall' anno 1457 sino all' anno 1500. *Bononiæ*, 1722, 4to

ORTLEPP (Ernst). Gedicht zum Gutenbergsfeste. *Leipzig*, 1840, 8vo

ORTLEPP (J. C.). Festgabe für den Deutschen Landmann. Eine Predigt auf Veranlassung der vierhundertjährigen Jubelfeier der Erfindung der Buchdruckerkunst am 2. Sonnt. nach Trin. 1840 in der Kirche zu Blumberg bei Torgan. *Halle*, 1840, 8vo

OSMONT (J. B. L.). Dictionnaire Typographique historique et critique des livres rares, singuliers, estimés et recherchés en tous genres. 2 vols. *Paris*, 1768, 8vo

OSTELL (W.). Ostell's Printer's Price Book, &c. *London*, 1856, 8º

OTT-USTERI. Eröffnungs-Rede der Jahres-Versammlung der Museum-Gesellschaft in Zurich am Jubelfeste der Erfindung der Buchdruckerkunst den 24 Juni 1840. *Zurich* [1840], 16mo

OTTINO (Giuseppe). Biblioteca Tipografica Italiana. 1871, 16mo

OTTINO (G.). Di Bernardo Cennini e dell' Arte della Stampa in Firenze nei primi cento anni dall' invenzione di essa, sommario storico, con documenti inediti. *Firenze*, 1871, 8*vo*

OTTINO (G.). La Stampa Periodica, il Commercio dei Libri e la Tipografia in Italia. *Milano*, 1875, *small folio*

OTTLEY (William Young). An Inquiry into the Origin and Early History of Engraving upon copper and in wood. With an account of Engravers and their works from the invention of Chalcography by Maso Finiguerra to the time of Marc' Antonio Raimondi. 2 vols. *London*, 1816, 4*to Large paper, the Perkins copy*

OTTLEY (W. Y.). An Inquiry concerning the Invention of Printing: in which the systems of Meerman, Heinecken, Santander, and Koning are reviewed; including also notices of the early use of wood engraving in Europe, the Block Books, &c. With an Introduction by J. Ph. Berjeau. *London*, 1863, 4*to*

OTTLEY (W. Y.). 129 Facsimiles of Scarce and Curious Prints illustrative of the History of Engraving. *London*, 1828, 4*to*

OTTLEY (W. Y.). 64 *Plates of facsimiles of Incunabula, watermarks, &c., apparently illustrating the proposed history of printing by Mr. Ottley*

OVEREND (Campbell). The noble printer and his adopted daughter, a tale of the first printed Bible. *Edinburgh*, 186-, 12*mo*

OXFORD. Friendly advice to the Correctour of the English Press at Oxford concerning the English Orthographie. *London*, 1682, *folio*. Reprinted from the Original with a Preface and Notes by William Sharswood. *London, printed at the Chiswick Press*, 1872, small 4°

OXFORD. A Specimen of the several sorts of Letter given to the University by Dr. John Fell, late Bishop of Oxford. To which is added the Letter given by Mr. F. Junius. *Oxford*, 1693, 8°

AEILE (Ch.). Essai Historique et Critique sur l'Invention de l'Imprimerie. *Paris*, 1859, 8*vo*

PAEILE (C.). Kritiesch Onderzoek naar de uitvinding der Boekdrukkunst ... oorspronkelijk in het Fransch bewerkt door J. H. Rutjes. *Amsterdam*, 1867, 8*vo*

PAITONI (Jac.). Venezia, la prima città, fuori della Germania, dove si esercito l' arte della Stampa, dissertazione. *Venezia*, 1772, 8°

PALIER. Iets over het geslacht der Palier's. [*No title*]. 8*vo*

PALLHAUSEN (Vincenz von). Denkmal in Stereotypen, den Manen Gutenberg's geweiht von Vincenz von Pallhausen im Jahre 1805 und zur vierten Säcularfeier der Buchdruckerkunst mit lithographirten Federzeichnungen zu Johannis 1836 herausgegeben von Progel. 1836, 4*to*

PALM (J. H. van der). Redevoering op het vierde eeuwfeest van de uitvinding der Boekdrukkunst binnen Haarlem, aldaar uitgesproken op den 10. Julij des jaars 1823. *Haarlem*, 1823, 8*vo*

PALMA DI BORGOFRANCO (Conte C.). Cenni su G. B. Bodoni. *Saluzzo*, 1872, 8°

PALMER (Edward). Glyphography or Engraved Drawing, for printing at the type press after the manner of woodcuts. Palmer's patent. *London*, 1843, 4*to*

PALMER (Samuel). The General History of Printing from its first invention in the City of Mentz, to its first progress and propagation thro' the most celebrated cities in Europe. Particularly, its introduction, rise and progress here in England. The Character of the most celebrated Printers, from the first Inventors of the Art to the years 1520 and 1550. With an Account of their Works, and of the most considerable Improvements which they made to it during that Interval. *London*, 1732, 4*to*, and 1733, 4*to*

Pangkofer (J. A.) und Schuegraf (J. R.). Geschichte der Buchdruckerkunst in Regensburg. *Regensburg*, 1840, 8vo

Panzer (Georg Wolfgang). Aelteste Buchdruckergeschichte Nürnbergs, oder Verzeichniss aller von Erfindung der Buchdruckerkunst, bis 1500 in Nürnberg gedruckten Bücher, mit literarischen Anmerkungen. *Nürnberg*, 1789, 4to

Panzer (G. W.). Annalen der ältern Deutschen Literatur.... von erfindung der Buchdruckerkunst bis 1526. 3 vols. in 2. *Nürnberg*, 1788—1805, 4to

Panzer (G. W.). Annales Typographici ab artis inventæ origine ad annum 1536, post Maittairii Denisii aliorumque curas in ordinem redacti et aucti. 11 vols. *Norimbergæ*, 1793—1803, 4°

Panzer (G. W.). Ausführliche Beschreibung der ältesten Augspurgischen Ausgaben der Bibel. *Nürnberg*, 1780, 4to

Panzer (G. W.). Geschichte der Nürnbergischen Ausgaben der Bibel. *Nürnberg*, 1778, 4to

Panzer (G. W.). Litterarische Nachricht von den allerältesten gedruckten Deutschen Bibeln aus dem 15 Jahrhundert. *Nürnberg*, 1777, 4to

Panzer (G. W.). Versuch einer kurzen Geschichte der romisch-catholichen Deutschen Bibelübersetzung. *Nürnberg*, 1781, 4to

Papillon (J. M.). Traité Historique et Pratique de la Gravure en Bois, ouvrage enrichi des plus jolis morceaux de sa composition et de sa gravure. 3 vols. *Paris*, 1766, 8vo

Parant (M.). Lois de la Presse en 1834. *Paris*, 1834, 8vo

Paris. Observations adressées à MM. les Imprimeurs de Paris, sur la Brochure intitulée: De l'Etat de l'Imprimerie Parisienne en 1854. *Paris*, 1854, 8°

Paris. Réponse des Imprimeurs de Paris à l'auteur de la Note sur la Constitution légale et sur la gestion administrative de l'Imprimerie Impériale. [*Paris*, 1864], 4to

Paris Exhibition, 1855. The Imperial Printing-Establishment at Vienna at the Universal Exhibition of Industry and Art at Paris, 1855. *Wien*, 1855, 8° *In German, English, Italian, and French*

PARKER (T.). A short Account of the first Rise and Progress of Printing, &c. *London*, 1763, 8º

PARKES (Mrs. Mary). The Electrotype as misapplied to Engraving in the National Art-Union. A Letter to Mr. Moon of Threadneedle Street. *London*, 1842, 8º

PAROY (Marquis de). Précis sur la Stéréotypie, précédé d'un coup d'oeil rapide sur l'origine de l'Imprimerie et de ses progrès. *Paris*, 1822, 8º

PARTINGTON (C. F.). The Engravers' Complete Guide; comprising the theory and practice of Engraving, with its modern improvements, in steel plates, lithography, &c. *London*, 1825, 8º

PARTINGTON (C. F.). The Printers' Complete Guide; containing a sketch of the History and Progress of Printing, to its present state of improvement; details of its several Departments; numerous schemes of Imposition; Modern Improvements in Stereotype, Presses and Machinery, &c., with Familiar Instructions to Authors, Illustrative of the Art of Correcting Proof Sheets. *London*, 1825, 8vo

PATENTS for Invention. Abridgements of the Specifications relating to Printing, including therein the production of copies on all kinds of materials (excepting felted and textile fabrics) by means of type, stereotype blocks, stone, dies, stencil plates, paper writings, electro-chemicals and light. *London*, 1859, cr. 8vo

PATER (Paulus). De Germaniæ miraculo optimo maximo, Typis Literarium, earumque differentiis, Dissertatio. *Lipsiæ*, 1710, 4to

PEIGNOT (Gabriel). Dictionnaire Raisonné de Bibliologie; contenant, 1º l'Explication des Termes relatifs à la Bibliographie, à l'Art Typographique . . . 2º des Notices Historiques . . . . sur les plus célèbres Imprimeurs, &c. 3 vols. *Paris*, 1802, 8º

PEIGNOT (G.). Essai historique sur la Lithographie, &c. *Paris*, 1819, 8º

PEIGNOT (G.). Notice sur la Lithographie. *Dijon*, 1818, 8º *Plates*

PEIGNOT (G.). Recherches historiques et bibliographiques sur les Imprimeries particulières et clandestines qui ont existé tant en France qu'à l'étranger depuis le XVe siècle jusqu'à nos jours, avec indication des principaux ouvrages sortis de ces sortes de presses. *Paris*, 1840, 8°

PELLEGRINI (Domenico Maria). Della prima Origine della Stampa in Venezia, per opera di Giovanni di Spira nel 1469 e risposta alla difesa del "Decor puellarum," dell' Abate Mauro Boni. *Venezia*, 1794, 8vo

PELLETIER (L.). La Typographie. Poëme. *Genève*, 1832, 8vo

PERICAUD (Antoine). Bibliographie Lyonnaise du XVe Siècle. Nouvelle édition. *Lyon*, 1851.—Bibliographie Lyonnaise du XVe Siècle, deuxième partie, contenant le Catalogue des Imprimeurs et des Libraires de Lyon de 1473 à 1500. *Lyon*, 1852.—Bibliographie Lyonnaise du XVe Siècle, troisième partie. *Paris, Lyon*, 1853, 8vo 200 *copies printed*

PERROT (A. M.). Manuel de Graveur; ou traité complet de l'art de la gravure en tous genres, d'après les renseignemens fournis par plusieurs artistes. *Paris*, 1830, 8° *Plates*

PESCHEK (H. E.). Der Ganze der Steindruckerei. 3. Aufl. *Weimar*, 1856, 8°

PETZHOLDT (Julius). Bibliotheca Bibliographica. Kritisches Verzeichniss der das gesammtgebiet der Bibliographie, betreffenden litteratur des in-und auslandes in systematischer ordnung. *Leipzig*, 1866, 8vo

PHILLIPS (G. F.). The Art of Drawing on Stone: in which is fully explained the process of chalk drawing, of pen and ink drawing, and of the dabbing system; together with the preparation of the ink and chalks. *London*, 1828, *sm.* 8°

PIC (F. A.). Code des Imprimeurs, Libraires, Ecrivains et Artistes ou Recueil et Concordance des dispositions législatives qui déterminent leurs obligations et leurs droits. 2 vols. *Paris*, 1826, 8vo

PICQUÉ (C.). Estienne Dolet. *Bruxelles, c.* 1860, 8°

PIERER. Druckproben der Hof-Buch-Druckerei in Altenburg. 1828, 4to

PIERRES (M). Description d'une Nouvelle Presse d'Imprimerie, approuvée par l'Académie Royale des Sciences et Imprimée sous son Privilège. *Paris*, 1786, 4to

PIERRON. Supplément à l'Instruction sur la Presse Autographique. *Paris*, 1830, 12°

PIETERS (Charles). Annales de l'Imprimerie des Elseviers. *Gand*, 1858, 8*vo*

PIIL (C.). Die Chemitypie, **oder die Kunst**, eine auf einer Metallplatte in gewöhnlicher Weise ausgeführte Radirung **oder Gravirung** in einen erhabenen Stempel zu verwandeln, der sich auf der Buchdruckerpresse, wie ein Holzschnitt, im Text oder allein, abdrucken lässt. *Leipzig*, 1846, 4*to*

PIJOLA (B.). **Del diritto concesso alla** Stamperia di Palermo nella sua fondazione. *Palermo*, 1822, 8°

PINCHART (A.). **Mémoire** sur les différentes Branches d'Industrie et de Commerce suivantes en 1776: 1°, **Caractères** à imprimer; 2°, **cartes à jouer**; 3°, livres, cartes géographiques, estampes **et tableaux**. [*Bruxelles*, 1850], 8*vo* *Only* **25** *copies printed from the " Bulletin du Bibliophile Belge," vol. viii*

PIPPING (Fredr. Wilh.). Några Historiska Underrättelser om Boktryckeriet i Finland [*pp.* 527—570 *of the Finnish Society's Transactions*, 1840; *and* 687—732 *of the same for* 1842]. *Helsingfors*, 4*to*

PISCHON (F. A.). **Kurze** Geschichte der Erfindung der Buchdruckerkunst **und** ihres segensreichen Einflusses. Einladung **zur** bevorstehenden vierhundertjährigen Gedächtnissfeier Gutenbergs und der Buchdruckerkunst am 24. Juni 1840 zunächt für die Schulen. *Berlin*, 1840, 8*vo*

PISCHON (F. A.). Von dem Einflusse der Erfindung der Buchdruckerkunst **auf** die Verbreitung des göttlichen **Worts**. Einladung zur sechs und zwanzigsten Stiftungsfeier der Preuzischen Haupt-Bibelgesellschaft **am** 21. Oktober 1840, nachtmittags 3 uhr in der Dreifaltigkeitskirche **zu** Berlin. [*Berlin*, 1840], 4*to*

PLAINE (François). Essai **Historique sur** les Origines et les Vicissitudes de l'Imprimerie en Bretagne. *Nantes*, 1876, 4*to* 100 *copies printed*

PLANTIN. **Index Librorum qui ex** Typographia Plantiniana **prodierunt.** *Antverpiæ*, 1615, 8*vo*

PLON (Henri). Fonderie, Imprimerie, Libraire. Quelques Mots sur les produits de la Maison Henri Plon. **Exposition** Universelle. *Paris*, 1855, 8°

POCH (Bernardo). Del Pentateuco stampato in Napoli (per impressores Soncinates) l'anno 1491, e Saggio di alcune varianti lezioni estratte da esso e da libri antichi della Sinagoga. *Roma*, 1780, 4°

Polluche (D.). Notices sur les imprimeurs de la ville d'Orléans, tiré d'une description MS. de la ville d'Orléans, par D. Polluche, Historiographe de cette ville, ob. 1768. *MS. copy by Mr. Bodel Nyenhuis, 7 pp. 4to*

Polypotype. Le Polypotype ou Histoire de l'Imprimerie sous la figure d'un Monstre. *Paris, 1827, 8°*

Porthmann (Jules). Essai Historique sur l'Imprimerie. *Paris, 1810, 8vo*

Pouy (Ferdinand). Recherches historiques sur l'Imprimerie et la Librairie à Amiens, avec une description de livres divers imprimés dans cette ville. *Amiens, 1861, 8vo*

Pozzoli (Giulio). Manuale di Tipografia ovvero guida pratica pei combinatori di caratteri, pei torcolieri e pei legatori di libri. *Milano, 1861, 8vo*

Pozzoli (G.). Nuovo Manuale di Tipografia, ossia Guida Pratica pei combinatori di caratteri, pei torcolieri, macchinisti, legatori di libri, ecc. Seconda Edizione migliorata ed accresciuta. *Milano, 1873, 8°*

Pozzoli (G.). Sull' uso dei fregi tipografici loro storia e progresso. 1871, 4°

Praet (J. B. B. Van). Notice sur Colard Mansion, Libraire et Imprimeur de Bruges. *Paris, 1829, 8vo Large and fine paper*

Praet (J. Van). Recherches sur la Vie, les Ecrits, et les Editions de Colard Mansion, imprimeur à Bruges durant le XVe siècle. *Paris, 1780, 8°*

Praloran (Giovanni). Delle origine e del primato della Stampa Tipografica. *Milano, 1868, 8vo*

Press (The) and the Public Service. *London, 1857, cr. 8vo*

Presswork. De nieuwe Corrector, onderrigtende, hoe, op eene gemakkelijke en voor mingeoefende vatbare manier, Druk-Proeven. *Rotterdam* [1800], 8vo

Preuschen (A. G.). Grundriss der Typometrischen Geschichte. *Basel, 1778, 8°*

Preusker (Karl). Gutenberg und Franklin. Eine Festgabe. *Leipzig, 1840, 8vo*

Printer (The). *London, 1833, 8°*

Printer (The). Henry and Huntington. Monthly. *New York, 1858, 4to*

Printer's Assistant (The). *London, 1810, 12mo*

Printer's Circular (The). A record of Typography, Literature, Arts, and Sciences. R. S. Menamin, Editor and Publisher. *Philadelphia,* 1866, *et seq.,* **sm.** 4*to*   *In progress*

Printer's Journal (The). Cincinnati Type Foundry, Quarterly. *Cincinnati,* 1871, 4*to*

Printer's Register (The). *London,* 1863, 4*to*
   In progress

Printing Times and Lithographer (The). *London,* 1875, 4*to*   *In progress*

Pront (Adrien). Elémens d'une typographie qui réduit au tiers celle en usage, et d'une écriture qui gagne près des trois quarts sur l'écriture françoise : l'une et l'autre fort agréables à la vue, applicables à toutes les Langues, conversant tous les principes grammaticaux et les richesses de celles qui s'impriment en caractère romain, et se rendent par l'écriture usitée en France ; fondées sur des principes simples et faciles à saisir, démontrées par des règles claires et précises ; dont on peut, en moins d'un jour, acquérir une parfaite théorie, qu'il est aisé d'apprendre, en très peu de temps, sans aucun secours étranger ; et dont l'écriture mettra une main habile en état de suivre la parole d'un orateur. *Paris,* 1797, 8*vo*

Proof Sheet (The). Monthly. Collins and McLeester. *Philadelphia,* 1867, 8*vo*

Psaume (Etienne). Bibliographie speciale et chronologique des principaux ouvrages sur l'Imprimerie et la Bibliologie. [*Supplement to his Dictionnaire Bibliographique,* tom. 1, *Paris,* 1824, 8°]

Pue (C.). Die Chemitypie. *Leipzig,* 1846, 4°

Putter (J. S.). Der Büchernachdruck nach ächten Grundsätzen des Rechts geprüft. *Gottingen,* 1774, 4°

Puy de Montbrun (E. P. J. du). Curiosités bibliographiques du 15e et 16e siècle, sorties des presses Néerlandaises. *Leide,* 1836, 8*vo*

Puy de Montbrun (E. P. J. du). Recherches bibliographiques sur quelques impressions néerlandaises du xve et du xvie siècle. *Leyde,* 1836, 8*vo*

QUADRAT (The). Monthly. A. C. Bakewell & Co. *Pittsburg, Penn.*, 1873, 8vo. *In progress*

QUANDT (Johann Gottlob von). Entwurf zu einer Geschichte der Kupferstecherkunst und deren Wechselwirkungen mit andern Zeichnenden Künsten. *Leipzig*, 1826, 16°

QUESTIONE (Sulla) della sciopero Tipografico. *Milano*, 1863, 8vo

QUIRINI (Ang. Mar.). Liber Singularis de optimorum scriptorum editionibus quæ Romæ primum prodierunt post divinum Typographiæ inventum, a germanis opificibus in eam urbem advectum : plerisque omnibus earum editionum seu præfationibus, seu epistolis in medium allatis. Cum brevibus observationibus ad easdem, rei typographicæ origini valde opportunis. Recensuit, annotationes, rerumque notabiliorum indicem adjecit, et diatribam præliminarem de variis rebus, ad natales artis typographicæ dilucidandos facientibus præmisit Jo. Greg. Schelhornius. *Lindaugiæ*, 1761, 4°

QUIRINI (A. M.). Specimen variæ literaturæ quæ in urbe Brixia ejusque ditione paulo post typographiæ incunabula florebat scilicet vergente ad finem Sæculo XV. usque ad medietatem Sæculi XVI. 2 parts. *Brixiæ*, 1739, 4to

RAFFELSBERGER (F.). Proben der ersten Geographischen Typen. *Wien*, 1838, 8°

RAMMELMAN ELSEVIER (W. J. C.). De Voormalige Drukkerij op het Raadhuis der Stad Leyden, 1577—1610. 1857, 8vo

RAMMELMAN ELSEVIER (W. J. C.). Uitkomsten van een onderzoek omtrent de Elseviers... Genealogie. *Utrecht*, 1845, 8vo *Not printed for sale*

RAPPORT van de Commissie, benoemd door den Raad der stad Haarlem, tot het onderzoek naar het jaar van de uitvinding der boekdrukkunst, en ter ontwerping van een plan voor de viering van het aanstaande eeuwfeest. *Haarlem*, 1822, 8*vo*

RAPPORTS faits à la Société d'Encouragement sur les Presses Mécaniques et celles à la Stanhope, de Giroudet, &c. *Paris*, 1834, 8°

RAREKES (Hendrik). Algemeene ophelderende verklaring van het Oud Letterschrift in Steenplaatdruk. Uitgegeven door de Maatschappij: tot nut van 't Algemeen. *Leyden*, 1818, 8° *And Atlas of* 17 *lithographic plates*, 4°

RATHGEBER (Georg). Annalen der Niederländischen Malerei, Formschneide-und Kupferstecherkunst. *Gotha*, 1842-44, *f*°

RATTWITZ (Carolus Fridericus). De Descriptione Typis Confecta cum in genere, tum quoad sigma musices in specie meditationes quædam, ex naturali potissimum jure deductæ. *Lipsiæ*, 1828, 4*to*

[RAUCOURT (   )]. A Manual of Lithography, or Memoir on the Lithographical Experiments made in Paris, at the Royal School of the Roads and Bridges; clearly explaining the whole Art as well as all the accidents that may happen in printing, and the different methods of avoiding them. Translated from the French by C. Hullmandel. *London*, 1820, 8*vo*

RAZOUMOFFSKY (Alexis). Notice des Monumens Typographiques qui se trouvent dans la Bibliothèque de Monsieur le Comte Alexis Razoumoffsky. *Moscou*, 1810, 8*vo*

REBER (Francis). De Primordiis artis imprimendi ac præcipue de Inventione Typographiæ Harlemensi. Dissertatio Inauguralis quam consensu et auctoritate amplissimi philosophorum ordinis in Alma literarium Universitate Friderica Guilelma ad summos in Philosophia Honores rite capessendos die IV. M. Augusti A. 1856, publice defendet. *Berolini*, 1856, 8*vo*

REED and Fox. Selections from the Specimen Book of the Fann Street Foundry. *London*, 8*vo*

REGT (J. K. de). Laurens Jansz. Koster, een blik op de uitvinding der Boekdrukkunst en op Haarlem, bij de aanstaande Feesten in Julij 1856. *Leyden*, 1856, 8*vo*

Regt (J. K. de). Lourens Jansz. Coster, of de Uitvinding der Boekdrukkunst; historisch drama met zang in 2 bedrijven en 3 tafereelen, met een naspel. *Leyden*, 1857, sm. 8º

Reichenbach (C.). Snelpersen-Fabriek. *Leyden*, 12mo

Reichhart (P. G.). Die Druckorte des XV Jahrhunderts, nebst Angabe der Erzeugnisse ihrer erstjährigen typographischen Wirksamkeit. *Augsburg*, 1853, 4to

Reiff (A.). De originibus typographicis. 3 parts. *Ingoldstadt*, 1785—90, 4º

Reiffenberg (Le Baron de). La plus ancienne Gravure connue avec une date. *Bruxelles*, 1845, 4to

Reinhardus (M. H.). De Typographia Torgaviensi illustri. Exponit et ad natalem tertium secularem Typographicæ artis aliquot oratiunculis celebrandum auditores humanissime invitat. 1740, 4º

Remfry (John). Specimens of Printing Types, Ornaments, &c. *London* [1840], 8vo

Renouard (A. A.). Alde l'ancien, Aldus Pius Romanus, et Henri Estienne, Henricus Stephanus Secundus. [*Paris*, 1838], 8º

Renouard (A. A.). Annales de l'imprimerie des Alde, ou Histoire des trois Manuce et de leurs éditions. *Paris*, 1834, 8vo *Large paper (32 copies printed) in 4to*

Renouard (A. A.). Annales de l'Imprimerie des Estienne ou histoire de la famille des Estienne et de ses éditions. *Paris*, 1837, 8º

Renouard (A. A.). Annales de l'Imprimerie des Estienne. Seconde édition. *Paris*, 1843, 8vo

Renouard (A. A.). Note sur Laurent Coster, à l'occasion d'un ancien livre imprimé dans les Pays Bas. [*Paris*, 1835], 8º

Renouard (A. A.). Notice sur la vie et les ouvrages des trois Manuce. *Paris*, 1803, 8º

Renouvier (Jules). Des Gravures en bois dans les livres d'Anthoine Verard, maître libraire, imprimeur, enlumineur et tailleur sur bois, de Paris, 1485—1512. *Paris*, 1859, 8vo *Only 200 copies printed*

Renouvier (J.). Des gravures sur bois dans les livres de Simon Vostre libraire d'Heures. Avec un avant-propos par Georges Duplessis. *Paris*, 1862, 8º

RENOUVIER (J.). Histoire de l'origine et des progrès de la Gravure dans les Pays-Bas et en Allemagne, jusqu'à la fin du quinzième siècle. *Bruxelles*, 1860, 8º

RENOUVIER (J.). Des Types et des Manières des Maîtres Graveurs, pour servir à l'histoire de la Gravure en Italie, en Allemagne, dans les Pays bas et en France. *Montpellier*, 1853-56, 4º

REPORT on King's Printers' Patents. *Bungay*, 1833, 8vo

REQUENO (Vincenzo). Osservazioni sulla Chirotipografia, ossia antica arte di Stampare a mano. *Roma*, 1810, 8º

REUME (A. de). Notes sur quelques Imprimeurs étrangers. *Bruxelles*, 1849, 8º

REUME (A. de). Notices Bio-Bibliographiques sur Imprimeurs, Libraires, &c. *Bruxelles*, 1858, 8vo

REUME (A. de). Recherches historiques, généalogiques, et Bibliographiques sur les Elsevier. *Bruxelles*, 1847, 8vo

REUSS (Eduard). Die Deutsche Historienbibel vor der Erfindung des Bücherdrucks. *Jena*, 1855, 8º

RINGWALT (J. Luther). American Encyclopædia of Printing. *Philadelphia*, 1871, *royal 8vo*

RITSCHL VON HARTENBACH (J.). Der Buchdruckerkunst Erfindung. Nebst einigen Betrachtungen über den Nutzen und die Nachtheile, welche seit ihrem Ursprunge aus ihrer verschiedenen Anwendung entstanden sind. *Sonderhausen*, 1820, 12mo

RITSCHL VON HARTENBACH (J.). Neues System Geographische Charten zugleich mit ihrem Colorit auf der Buchdruckerpresse herzustellen. *Leipzig*, 1840, 8vo

RIVE (M. l'Abbé). Prospectus d'un Ouvrage proposé par souscription. [Histoire de la Peinture et de la Caligraphie]. *12mo*

RIVE (M.). Eclaircissements historiques et critiques sur l'Invention des cartes à jouer. *Paris*, 1780, 12mo

RIVINUS (Andreas). Hecatomba Laudum et Gratiarum, ob Inventam in Germaniæ abhinc annis c c calcographiam . . . . Artis Typographicæ Commendationem. *Lipsiæ*, 1640, 4º

ROBIN (Ch.). Histoire Illustrée de l'Exposition Universelle. 1ʳᵉ Partie [*Printing, Type Founding, &c.*]. *Paris*, 1855, 8vo

ROEST (M.). De "Wetenschappelijke moraliteit" van Dr. A. Van der Linde. *Amsterdam*, 1870, 8vo

ROME. Specimen Characterum Typographiæ S. Consilii Christiano Nomini Propagundo SS. D. N. Gregorio XVI. Pont. Max. idem Typographeum invisenti. *Roma*, 1842, f°

ROORDA (P.). Berigt en Proeve van de Nieuwe Javansche Drukletters, &c. *Haarlem*, 1839, 4°

RORET (M.). Nouveau Manuel Complet de l'Imprimeur Lithographe, avec Atlas. *Paris*, 1830, 12°

ROSELL Y TORRES. Noticia. 1873, 8°

ROSENBUSCH (C. E.). Einige Schriftproben und Verzierungen. *Göttingen*, 8vo

ROSSI (Johann Bernard de). Annales Hebræotypographici sec. XV descripsit fusoque commentario illustravit. *Parmæ*, 1795, 4to

ROSSI (J. B. de). Annales Hebræo-typographici ab anno 1501 ad annum 1540. Digessit notis que hist. criticis instruxit. *Parmæ*, 1799, 4°

ROSSI (J. B. de). Annali Ebreo-Tipografici di Cremona. *Parma*, 1808, 8vo

ROSSI (J. B. de). Annali Ebreo-tipografici di Sabionetta sotto Vespasian Gonzaga, distesi ed illustrati. *Parma*, 1780, 4°

ROSSI (J. B. de). De Hebraicae Typographiae origine ac primitiis, seu antiquis ac rarissimis Hebraicorum Librorum editionibus seculi XV. Disquisitio Historico-Critica. Recudi curavit M. Guilielmus Fridericus Hufnagel. *Erlangæ*, 1778, 8vo

ROSSI (J. B. de). De Typographia Hebraeo-Ferrariensis Commentarius historicus, quo Ferrarienses Judaeorum Editiones Hebraicae, Hispanicae, Lusitanae recensentur et illustrantur. *Parmæ*, 1780, 8vo

ROSSI (J. B. de). Dell' Origine della Stampa in Tavole Incise e di una antica e sconosciuta edizione zilografica. *Parma*, 1811, 8vo

ROTH-SCHOLTZIUS (Frid.). Icones Bibliopolarum et Typographorum de republica litteraria benè meritorum, ab incunabulis typographiæ ad nostra usque tempora. *Norimbergæ et Altorfii*, 1726-42, f°

ROTH-SCHOLTZIUS (F.). Thesaurus symbolorum ac emblematum, id est insignia bibliopolarum et typographorum, accedit Geo. And. Vinholdi programma de quibusdam notis et insignibus bibliopolarum et typographorum. *Norimbergæ et Altorfii*, 1730, *folio*

ROUND'S Printers' **Cabinet.** S. P. Round. Quarterly. *Chicago*, 1857, *folio*

ROUSSELLE (Hippolyte). Bibliographie Montoise. Annales de l'imprimerie à Mons, depuis 1580 jusqu'à **nos jours.** *Mons*, 1858, *royal* 8*vo Large paper*

RUDOLPH (E. C.). Die Buckdrucker-Familie Froschauer in Zurich, **1521**—1595. Verzeichniss der aus ihrer offizin hervorgegangenen **Druckwerke.** *Zurich*, **1869,** 8*vo*

RUDOLPH (Herrmann). Kurze Geschichte der Erfindung der Buchdruckerkunst im **Jahre 1440.** Eine Vorbereitungsschrift **auf die vierte** Säcularfeier dieser Erfindung im **Jahre** 1840, für Schule und Haus. *Meissen*, 1840, **12***mo*

RUEDA (Manuel de). Instruccion para Gravar en Cobre, y perfeccionarse en el gravado à buril, al agua fuerte, y al humo, con el nuovo methodo de gravar las planchas para estampar en colores, à imitacion de la Pintura; y un compendio Historico de los mas célebres Gravadores, que se han conocido desde su invencion hasta el presente. *Madrid*, 1761, **12**º

RUELENS (Charles). **Un incunable** anglais inconnu. [*Bruxelles*, 1865], 8*vo With facsimile. Reprinted from the " Annales du Bibliophile Belge "*

RUELENS (C.). Un plaidoyer **nouveau pour Laur.** Coster. (*Brux. c.* 1860), 8º

RUELENS (C.). **La** question de l'origine de l'Imprimerie et la grand Concile Typographique. *Bruxelles*, 1855, 8º *Fifty copies printed separately from the " Bulletin du Bibliophile Belge "*

RUELENS (C.) et BACKER (A. de). Annales Plantiniennes, depuis la fondation de l'Imprimerie Plantinienne à Anvers jusqu'à la mort de Ch. Plantin (1555—1589). *Paris*, 1866, 8*vo*

RUMOHR (C. F. von). Zur Geschichte und Theorie der Formschneidekunst. *Leipzig*, 1837, 8º

RUSE (Geo.). Imposition simplified. *London*, 187—, 18*mo*

RUSKIN (John). Ariadne Florentina. Six Lectures on Wood and Metal Engraving, given before the

University of Oxford, in Michaelmas term, 1872.
6 parts. *Orpington, 1873-75, 8vo*

RUTHVEN. A short account of Lithography, or the Art of printing from Stone. *Edinburgh, 1820, 8°*

SAINT-ARROMAN (Raoul de). La Gravure à l'eau forte, essai historique. Comment je devins graveur à l'eau forte, par le Comte LEPIC. *Paris, 1876, 8vo*

SAINT GEORGES (M. de). Notice Historique sur l'Imprimerie Nationale. *Paris, 1851, 8°*

SAINT PAUL (F. B.). Nouveau Système Typographique, dont les expériences ont été faites en 1775 aux frais du Gouvernement; ou Moyen de diminuer de moitié, dans toutes les imprimeries de l'Europe, le travail et les frais de composition, de correction et de distribution, decouvert en 1774, par Madame .... *Paris, 1776, 4°*

ST. PETERSBURG. Specimen Book of the Printing Office and Type Foundry of the Imperial Academy of Science [in Russian.] *Catherinopolo, St. Petersburg, 1861, royal 8°*

ST. PETERSBURG. Specimen Book of the Printing Office and Type Foundry of the Imperial Academy of Science at St. Petersburg. Edited by Ph. Hagel [in Russian]. *Catherinopolo [St. Petersburgh], 1870, royal 4°*

SALMON (William). Polygraphice; or the Arts of drawing, engraving, etching, limning, painting, washing, varnishing, colouring and dying. 2 vols. *London, 1701, 12mo*

SALVIONI (Giuseppe). Cenni storici sulla zilografia ossia incisione in legno, seguiti da alcune considerazioni intorno alle attuali condizioni di quest' arte in Italia. *Torino, 1868, 8vo*

SALVO-Cozzo (Giuseppe). Osservazioni sulla questione del primato della Stampa tra Palermo e Messina. *Palermo, 1874, 8vo*

Sanlecques. Epreuves des Caractères du Fond des Sanlecques. *Paris*, 1757, 12°

Santander (C. de la Serna). Dictionnaire Bibliographique Choisi du quinzième siècle. 3 vols. *Bruxelles*, 1805-7, 8vo

Santander. Essai Historique sur l'origine de l'Imprimerie ainsi que sur l'histoire de son établissement dans les Villes, Bourgs, Monastères, et autres endroits de l'Europe; avec la Notice des Imprimeurs qui y ont exercé cet art jusqu'à l'an 1500. *Bruxelles*, 1805, 8°

Santander. An Historical Essay on the Origin of Printing, translated from the French. *Newcastle*, 1819, 8vo 160 *copies printed, of which* 30 *were on large paper*

Santander. Mémoire sur l'Origine et le premier Usage des Signatures et des Chiffres dans l'Art Typographique. *Bruxelles, an IV* (1796), 8vo

Sardini (Giacomo). Congetture sopra un' antica stampa, trasmesse ultimamente in tre lettere ad Anton Maria Amoretti, ed ora pubblicate dal Ferdinando Fossi. *Firenze*, 1793, 4to

Sardini (G.). Esame sui principii della Francese ed Italiana Tipografia, ovvero Storio critica di Nicolò Jenson. 3 parts. *Lucca*, 1796-98, *folio*. 5 *plates*

Saunders (Frederic). Authors' Printing and Publishing Assistant, including details respecting the Mechanism of books. *New York*, 1839, 12mo

Savage (William). Dictionary of the Art of Printing, embodying the whole theory and practice of the Art of Typography brought down to the present day. *London*, 1841, 8vo

Savage (W.). On the Preparation of Printing Ink; both black and coloured. *London*, 1832, 8°

Savage (W.). Practical Hints on Decorative Printing, with illustrations engraved on wood and printed in colours at the type press. *London*, 1822, 4to

Saxe (Joseph Antonio). Historia literario-typographica Mediolanensis in qua, de studiis literariis antiquis et novis in hac Metropoli institutis. De tempore inductæ Mediolanum Typographiæ: et primis hujus artis Opificibus, &c. *Mediolani*, 1745, *folio*. (*This work forms the first vol. of P.*

Argelati Bibliotheca Scriptorum Mediolanensium, 4 vols. *folio*)

SCARABELLI (L.). Di **Panfilo Castaldi**. **Lettera** all' abate Bernardi. *Bologna,* 1866, 8°

SCHAAB (C. A.). Die Geschichte der erfinding der Buchdruckerkunst durch Joh. Gensfleisch genannt Gutenberg zu Mainz, pragmatisch aus den Quellen bearbeitet, mit mehr als drittalb Hundert noch ungedruckten Urkunden, welche die Genealogie Gutenberg's, Fust's, und Schöffer's in ein neues Licht stellen. 3 vols. *Mainz,* 1831, 8vo

SCHAAB (C. A.). Randglossen zu den Phantasien und Träumereien des Pseudogeistes Johann Gensfleisch, genannt Gutenberg, an Dr. C. A. Schaab und den Ausschutz zur Errichtung des Denkmals zu seiner Ehre zu Mainz, Utrecht bei Robert Natan und gedruckt zu Haag, 1835. Mit zwei Anhängen: I. Historischer Beweis, dass die vierte Jubelfeier der Erfindung der Buchdruckerkunst in dem laufenden Jahre 1836 eintrete und nicht im Jahre 1840, oder einem andern könne gefeiert werden. II. Ueber die Monumentssache und was seit dreissig Jahren darin geschehen ist. *Mainz,* 1836, 8vo

SCHAAFF (J. H. van der). Verhandeling over het nut der Boekdrukkunst. Voorgelezen in de Zutphensche Afdeeling der Maatschappij: tot nut van 't Algemeen den 5den van Slagtmaand, 1823. *Amsterdam,* 1823, 8°

SCHAEFER (J. W.). Historischer Bericht von der Buchdruckerkunst. *Bremen,* 1840, 8vo

SCHEIBEL (Johann **Ephraim**). Geschichte der seit dreihundert Jahren in Breslau befindlichen Stadtbuchdruckerey, als ein Beitrag zur allgemeinen Geschichte der Buchdruckerkunst. *Breslau,* 1804, 4to

SCHELHORNIUS. De Antiquissima Latinorum Bibliorum editione ceu primo Artis Typographicæ. *Ulmæ,* 1760, *small* 4to

SCHELTEMA (Jacobus). Bericht und Beurtheilung der Werkes von Dr. C. A. Schaab betitelt: Die Geschichte der Erfindung der Buchdruckerkunst, durch Johann Gensfleisch, genannt Gutenberg zu Mainz. *Amsterdam,* 1833, 8vo

SCHELTEMA (J.). Berigt en beordeeling van het werk van Mr. C. A. Schaab: De Geschiedenis der Uitvinding van Boekdrukkunst. *Utrecht,* 1832, 8º

SCHELTEMA (J.). Conspectus of berigt aangaande de verhandeling van Jacobus Koning, over de uitvinding, verbetering en volmaking der Boekdrukkunst. *Amsterdam,* 1817, 8vo

SCHELTEMA (J.). De geloofwaardigheid van Adrianus Junius gehandhaafd, ten opzigte van zijne berigten aangaande de Uitvinding en Beoefening der Boekdrukkunst te Haarlem. [*Haarlem*], 1834, 8º *Portrait of Junius*

SCHELTEMA (J.). Der geist Johann Genfleisch's genannt Gutenberg an Dr. C. A. Schaab. Und den ausschuss zur errichtung des denkmales zu seiner ehre zu Mainz. *Utrecht,* 1835, 8vo

SCHELTEMA (J.). Lettre à MM. les rédacteurs de la Galerie des Contemporains sur la nécessité de rectifier et completter l'article concernant M. J. Koning. *La Haye,* 1819, 8vo

SCHELTEMA (J.). Over het werk: Bartholomeus Engelschman (*Glanvilla*), Proprieteiten d. dingen. Haarl. 1485.—Beoordeeling v. het werk v. Schaab.—Levensschets van Laurens Janszoon Koster. [*Utrecht*], 1834, 8vo

SCHELTEMA (J.) en KONING (J.). Vier breven gewisseld tusschen over de laatste tegenspraak van het regt van Haarlem op de Uitvinding der Drukkunst. *Haarlem,* 1823, 8vo

SCHEURMANN. Printing music. *London,* 1856, 8º

SCHIER (X.). Commentatio de Primis Vindobonæ Typographis. *Vindobonæ,* 1764, 4to

SCHINKEL (A. D.). Beschrijving van een Triptikon en een Diptikon. *'s Grav.,* 1845, 8vo *Not printed for sale*

SCHINKEL (A. D.). Beschrijving van het in de Koninklijke Bibliotheek te 's Gravenhage berustende Handschrift der Batavia, uit de nagelaten schriften van Mr. Gerard van Lennep. *'s Gravenhage,* 1840, 8vo *Not printed for sale*

SCHINKEL (A. D.). Beschrijving van twee prachtexemplaren over de uitvinding der Boekdrukkunst. 1848, 8vo [*Privately printed*]

SCHINKEL (A. D.). Geschied-en Letterkundige Bijdragen, met twee facsimiles. *'s Gravenhage,* 1850, 8vo *125 copies printed, not for sale*

SCHINKEL (A. D.). Handschriften en oude drukken (incunabelen) deel uitmakende van de kunst-en letter-verzamelingen. *'s Hage*, 1853, 8vo *Only 150 copies printed*

SCHINKEL (A. D.). Hedendaagsche voorstelling van Coster en de uitvinding der Boekdrukkunst in Frankrijk. Uitgegeven ten voordeele der oprigting van een standbeeld voor Lourens Jansz. Coster. *'s Gravenhage*, 1853, 8vo

SCHINKEL (A. D.). Tweetal Bijdragen betrekkelijk de Boekdrukkunst. *'s Gravenhage*, 1844, 8vo *Privately printed*

SCHLEGEL (Dr.). Geschichte Gutenberg's und seiner grossen Erfindung, für das Deutsche Volk bearbeitet. *Leipzig*, 1840, 32mo

SCHLETTER (H. T.). Handbuch der deutschen Press-Gesetzgebung. *Leipzig*, 8°

SCHLOTKE (F.). Das Mappen der Buchdruckerkunst in Typographischen Farbendruck. *Bonn*, 1857, 1858, 8°

SCHMALTZ (J. C. St.). Das Jubiläum der Buchdruckerkunst im Jahre 1840. Nebst geschichtlichen Nachrichten über die Jubelfeiern in den Jahren 1540, 1640, und 1740, und Ankündigung eines Lexikon's sämmtlicher Buchhändler und Buchdrucker, von Erfindung der Buchdruckerkunst an. *Quedlinburg*, 1836, 8vo

SCHMATZ (D. M.). Neu vorgestelltes auf der löblichen Kunst Buchdruckerey gebräuchliches Format Buch. *Sulzbach*, 1684, 8°

SCHMID (A.). Ottaviano dei Petrucci da Fossombrone, der erste Erfinder des Musiknotendruckes mit beweglichen Metalltypen, und seine Nachfolger im sechszehnten Jahrhunderte. *Wien*, 1845, 8°

SCHMID (A. E. von). Abdruck der Schriften. *Wien*, 1827, 4to

SCHMIDT (Johannes). Drey Christliche danck Predigten: wegen dero im Jahr 1440 ...... in Strassburg erfundenen hochwerthen thewren Buchtruckerkunst. *Strassburg*, 1641, 4to

SCHMIDT (J.). Gott zu Lob. Drey Christliche Danck-Predigten: wegen dero im Jahr 1440, und also vor zweyhundert Jahren, durch Göttliche eingebung, in Strassburg erfundenen Hochwerthen thewren Buchtruckerkunst: nach Anleitung dess andern versiculs des iii. Psalms "Gross findt die Wercke des Herrn, wer ihrachtet der hat eitel Lust daran" in volckreicher Versamlung zu Strassburg anno 1640 den 18, 25 Augusti und 1 Septembr. gehalten, und, auff begehren, in Truck gegeben. *Gotha, 1740, small 8vo* (*On pp. 109 to 127 are printed* "*J. H. Boecleri Oratio de Typographiæ Argentorati inventæ, divinitate et satis, Sæculari pietate disseritur," as delivered in October*, 1640)

SCHNURRER (C. F.). Programm zur Geschichte der Tübingischen Typographie. *Tübingen*, 8º

SCHNURRER (C. F.). Slavischer Bücherdruck in Wurtemberg im 16 Jahrhundert. *Tübingen*, 1799, 8vo

SCHÖBER (David Gottfried). Ausführlicher Bericht von alten deutschen geschriebenen Bibeln, vor Erfindung der Buchdruckerey nebst einem alt deutschen Bibl. Wort-Register, aus einer alten geschriebenen deutschen Bibel und deren Beschreibung. *Schleiz, 1763, small 8vo*

SCHOEPFLIN (Jo. Daniel). Vindiciæ Typographicæ. *Argentorati*, 1760, 4to

SCHOOK (C.). Handboekje voor Letterzetters, Boekdrukken, en Correctors. *Gorinchem*, 1860, 12mo

SCHRAG (Adam). Bericht von der Buchdrukkerey. *Strasburg*, 1640, 4º

SCHREIBER (T. J.). Erstlinge der Jubelfeyer in Dantzig wegen der vor 300 Jahren erfunding Buchdruckerey. 1740, 4to

SCHRŒDER (I. H.). Incunabula artis typographicæ in Suecia. *Upsaliæ*, 1842, 4to

SCHRŒDER (Dr. W.). Album des Gutenberg-Festes zu Hannover im Jahre 1840. *Hannover*, 1840, 8vo

SCHROENIUS (W. A.). Occasione Novæ quæ Constantinopoli est exstructa Typographiæ. *Vinariæ*, 1731, sm. 4to

SCHUCK (Julius). Aldus Manutius und seine Zeitgenossen, in Italien und Deutschland. Im Anhange: die Familie der Aldus bis zu ihrem Ende. *Berlin*, 1861, 8º

SCHULZ (Otto August). Gutenburg, oder Geschichte der Buchdruckerkunst. *Leipzig*, 1840, 8vo

SCHULZE (Christian Ferdinand). Wechselwirkung zwischen der Buchdruckerkunst und der Fortbildung der Menschheit. Eine Rede am Jubelfest der Erfindung der Buchdruckerkunst den 24. Juni 1840 gehalten im Gymnasium zu Gotha. *Gotha* [1840], 8vo

SCHULZE (J. G.). Programme de Officina typographica Constantinopoli instituta. *Norimbergæ*, 1728, 4º

SCHUMANN (Carl). Schrift Proben der Buchdruckerei. *Schneeberg*, 1828, 4to

SCHWABE (C. L.). Die Erfindung der Buchdruckerkunst und ihre folgen. Eine vorbereitungschrift zur vierten Säkularfeier. *Leipzig*, 1840, 12mo

SCHWARZ (Ch. Gott.). De ornamentis librorum apud veteres usitatis, disputationes duas. *Lipsiæ*, 1705, 4to

SCHWARZ (J. C. E.). Predigt zum Gedächtniss der Erfindung der Buchdruckerkunst am ersten Sonntage nach Trinitatis in der Stadtkirche zu Jena. *Jena*, 1840, 8vo

SCHWARZ (J. L.). Der Buchdrucker. *Hamburg, Leipzig*, 1775, 8º

SCHWETSCHKE (Gustav). De Donati minoris fragmento Halis nuper reperto. *Halis*, 1839, 4to

SCHWETSCHKE (G.). Vorakademische Buchdruckergeschichte der Stadt Halle. *Halle*, 1840, 8vo

SCOTT (William B.). Albert Dürer, his life and works. *London*, 1869, 8º

SCRIVERIUS (Peter). Laure-crans voor Laurens Coster van Haerlem, eerste vinder vande Boeck-Druckery. *Haerlem*, 1628, 4to

SCULPTURA-HISTORICO-TECHNICA: or the History and Art of Engraving. Containing, I. The Rise and Progress of Engraving. II. Of Engraving in General. III. Of Engraving, Etching, and Scraping on Copper as now practised. IV. An Idea of a fine Collection of Prints. V. The Repertorium or a Collection of various Marks and Cyphers, with additions. To which is now added a chronological and historical series of the Painters from the Eleventh Century. Extracted from Baldinucci, Florent le Compte, Faithorne, the Abecedario Pittorico, and other authors. With copper plates. The Fourth Edition. *London*, 1770, cr. 8vo

SEELEN (Joh. Henr. von). Nachricht von dem Ursprung und Fortgang der Buchdruckerey in der Reichs-Stadt Lubeck, worinn die Lubeckischen Buchdrucker und allerley von Ihnen gedruckte merckwürdige Bücher und Schrifften angeführet und beschrieben werden. Bey Gelegenheit des iu diesem 1740sten Jahre einfallenden Buchdrucker-Jubilaei ertheilet, und mit verschiedenen zur Gelehrten Historie gehörigen Anmerckungen. *Lubeck,* 1740, *8vo*

SEEMILLER (Sebastian). Bibliothecæ Academicæ Ingoldstadiensis Incunabula Typographica. 2 vols. in 1. *Ingoldstadii,* 1787, *4to*

SEIZ (John Christian). Het derde Jubeljaar der uitgevondene Boekdrukkunst door Laurens Janz. Koster. Het derde Jubeljaar der uitgevondene Boekdrukkunst, behelzende een beknopt Historis Verhaal van de Uitvinding der Edele Boekdrukkunst. *Haerlem,* 1740, *8vo, plates*

SEIZ (J. C.). Annus Sæcularis Tertius inventæ Artis Typographicæ à Laurentio Kostero, Cive et Senatore Civitatis Harlemensis. Ex idiomate Belgico in gratiam exterorum Latine et hinc inde auctior reddita. *Harlemi,* 1742, *8°*

SEMLER (Joh. Salomo). Sammlungen zur Geschichte der Formschneidekunst in Teutschland. *Leipzig,* 1782, *8vo*

SENEFELDER (Aloys). L'Art de la Lithographie, ou Instruction pratique contenant la description claire et succincte des différens procédés à suivre pour dessiner, graver et imprimer sur pierre; précédée d'une Histoire de la Lithographie et de ses divers progrès. *Paris,* 1819, *4to Portrait and atlas of 20 plates*

SENEFELDER (A.). Complete Course of Lithography. *London,* 1819, *4to*

SENEFELDER (A.). Lehrbuch der Lithographie, &c. *Regensburg,* 1834, *8°*

SENEFELDER (A.). Vollständeges Lehrbuch der Steindruckerey. *München,* 1827, *4to*

SHACKELL and LYONS. Specimen of Printing Inks. *London, 8vo*

SHARWOOD (S. and T.). Annual Catalogue of Printing Materials. *London,* 1855-6, *8vo*

SHAW (Henry). A Handbook of the Art of Illumination as practised during the Middle Ages. With a description of the metals, pigments, and processes employed by the artists at different periods. *London,* 1866, *impl. 4to*

SHERMAN (A. N.). The Printers' Manual; or a Brief Practical Treatise on the Art of Printing, including some new and important subjects not before discovered. *New York*, 1834, 16*mo*

SIENNICKI (Stanislas Joseph). De Typographia in Claro Monte Czenstochoviensi Librisque in ejusdem officina ab anno 1628 usque ad 1864 impressis. *Varsoviæ*, 1873, 12*mo Not printed for sale*

SILBERMANN (G.). Album Typographique, publié à l'occasion de la quatrième fête séculaire de l'Invention de l'Imprimerie. *Strasbourg*, 1840, 4*to Plates and cuts*

SILVESTRE (L. C.). Marques Typographiques, ou recueil des Monogrammes, Chiffres, Enseignes, Emblèmes, Devises, Rébus et Fleurons des Libraires et Imprimeurs qui ont exercé en France, depuis l'introduction de l'Imprimerie en 1470, jusqu'à la fin du seizième siècle : à ces marques sont jointes celles des Libraires et Imprimeurs qui pendant la même période ont publié, hors de France, des Livres en langue Française. *Paris*, 1853-67, 8*vo*

SIMON (C. F.). Projet de l'Etablissement d'une Imprimerie à Berlin. *Paris*, 1741, *f°*

SIMONEAU (Louis). Recueil d'Estampes gravées en taille douce pour servir à l'histoire de l'art de l'Imprimerie et de Gravure. 1694, *f°*

SINAPIUS (Dan. Aug.). Apparatus ad Pauli Manutii vitam. *Lipsiæ*, 1719, 4°

SINCLAIR (Duncan) and SONS. Specimen of Modern Printing Types cast at the Letter Foundery of Whiteford House, Edinburgh. 1840, 4*to*

SINCLAIR and SONS' Specimens of Modern Printing Types. *Edinburgh*, 1842, 4*to*

SINGER (Samuel Weller). Researches into the History of Playing Cards, with Illustrations of the Origin of Printing and Engraving on Wood. *London*, 1816, 4*to*

SINGER (S. W.). Some account of the book printed at Oxford in 1468. *London*, 1812, 8*vo*

SKEEN (William). Early Typography. An Essay on the Origin of Letter Press Printing in the Fifteenth Century. *London*, 1872, 8*vo* [*Printed at Colombo, Ceylon*]

SKEEN (W.). Typography or Letter Press Printing in the Fifteenth Century. A Lecture. *Colombo, Ceylon*, 1853, 8*vo*

SMITH (John). The Printer's Grammar. *London,* 1755, 8*vo*

SMITS (J.). Iets over de uitvinding der Boekdrukkunst. *Dordrecht,* 1856, 8*vo*

SNELLEN (Dr. H.). Letterproeven, totbepaling der gezigtsscherpte. *Utrecht,* 1862, 8*vo*

SOHM (Peter). Musaeum Typographicum Sohmianum, eller Förteckning på de Böcker och Skrifter om Boktryckeri-Konsten och dess Historia, jemte Portraiter af namnkunnige Boktryckare, samt Medailler i samme Amne. 2 parts. *Stockholm,* 1812-15, 8°

SORGATO (D. Gaetano). Della Stamperia del seminario di Padova: Memoria. *Padova,* 1843, 8*vo*

SOTHEBY (Samuel Leigh). Memoranda relating to the Block-Books preserved in the Bibliothèque Impériale, Paris. *London, Printed for the Author,* 1859, 4*to*

SOTHEBY (S. L.). Principia Typographica. The Block Books, or Xylographic delineations of Scripture History, issued in Holland, Flanders, and Germany during the 15th Century, exemplified and considered in connexion with the origin of Printing. To which is added an attempt to elucidate the character of the paper marks of the period. A work contemplated by the late Samuel Sotheby, and carried out by his son, S. L. S. 3 vols. *London,* 1858, 4*to*

SOTHEBY (S. L.). Typography of the Fifteenth Century: being specimens of the productions of the early Continental Printers, exemplified in a collection of fac-similes from one hundred works, together with their water marks. Arranged and edited from the bibliographical collections of the late S. S., by his son S. Leigh Sotheby. *London,* 1845, *folio*

SOTZMANN. Aelteste Geschichte der Xylographie und der Druckkunst überhaupt, besonders in der Anwendung auf den Bilddruck. Ein Beitrag zur Erfindungs-und Kunstgeschichte. [1837], 12*mo*

SOTZMANN. Ueber die gedruckten *Literæ Indulgentiarum Nicolai V. Pont. M. pro Regno Cypri* von 1454 und 1455. *Leipzig,* 1844, 8*vo, fac-simile plate*

SOUQUET (G.). Mémoire sur un nouvel instrument nommé *Justificateur,* inventé par G. Souquet. *Boulogne-sur-Mer,* 1824, 8°

SPANISH ROYAL PRESS. Muestras de los nuevos Punzones y Matrices para la letra de Imprenta. 1787, 8*vo*

SPANO (G.). Notizie storiche documentate intorno á Niccolò Canelles della città d'Iglesias, primo introduttore dell' arte tipografica in Sardegna. *Cagliari*, 1866, 8º

SPECIMEN Typographique de l'Imprimerie Royale. *Paris*, 1845, *f*º

[SPILSBURY (F.)]. The Art of Etching and Aquatinting, strictly laid down by the most approved masters; sufficiently enabling Amateurs in Drawing to transmit their Works to Posterity; or as Amusements among their Circle of Friends. To which is added the most useful Liquid Colours, well adapted for staining and colouring the above, &c. &c. with a specimen of Landscape and Profile by F. Yrubslips. *London*, 1794, 12º

SPIN (C. A.). Drukproef met onderscheidene Lettersoorten uit de Drukkerij van C. A. S. *Amsterdam*, 1825, 4*to*

SPOERLIUS (Johannis Conradi). Introductio in Notitiam Insignium Typographicorum. Dissertatione Epistolari ad Fridericum Roth-Scholtzium proposita. *Norimbergæ et Altorfii*, 1730, 4*to*

SPRENGER (P. P.). Aelteste Buchdruckergeschichte von Bamberg. *Nürnberg*, 1800, 4*to*

STANBURY (G.). Practical Guide to Lithography, or the Art of Drawing on Stone; and the various uses of the Materials supplied by him. *London*, 1854, 8º

STANGLEN (Karl). Kurze Geschichte der Buchdruckerkunst seit ihrer Erfindung bis auf die neueste zeit, nebst den Biographien einiger der berühmtesten Buckdrucker. Aus den sichersten Quellen geschöpft. *Stuttgart*, 1840, 12*mo*

STAPART. L'Art de Graver au pinceau, nouvelle méthode qu'on peut excécuter sans avoir l'habitude au burin. *Paris*, 1773, 12º

STARCKE (Petrus). De Ortu Typographiæ. 1666, 4*to*

STARK (Adam). Printing; Its antecedents, origin, history, and results. *London*, 1855, 8*vo*

STARKLOF (L.). Drei Tage in Mainz am Gutenbergsfeste. Eine Skizze. *Mainz*, 1837, 12*mo*

STATIONERS' COMPANY. A transcript of the Registers of the Stationers' Company of London, edited by

Edward Arber, F.S.A. Vol. 1, 2, 3, (July, 1876). *Privately printed. London*, 1874-6, 4º

STATIONERS' COMPANY. The Charter and Grants of the Company of Stationers of the City of London now in force, containing a plain and rational account of the Freemen's Rights and Privileges, fairly produced and where necessary, impartially explain'd. In order to ascertain the Authority annexed to the Office of Master and Wardens and to redress the Hardships and Miseries of the injured and oppressed Freemen. To which is added an Appendix: shewing that the Court of Assistants was imposed upon the Freemen by a Charter granted by Charles II. which, because it was found unreasonable, oppressive and illegal, was revoked and made null and void by an Act of Parliament in the 2 W. & M. &c. *London*, 1741, 12º

STAVEREN (J. S. van). Redevoering voor de Kinderen der Stads-Armen-Scholen, bij gelegenheid van het vierde eeuwgetijde van de uitvinding der Boekdrukkunst door Laurens Jansz. Koster. Gehouden binnen Haarlem den 11 Julij 1823. *Haarlem*, 1823, 12mo

STEIGENBERGER (Gerhoh). Historisch-Literarisches Versuch von entstehung und aufnahme der kurfurstlichen Bibliothek in München. 1784, 4to

STEIGENBERGER (G.). Literarisch-Kritische Abhandlung über die zwo allerälteste gedruckte deutsche Bibeln. *München*, 1787, *small* 4to

STEPHANUS (Henricus). Epistola, qua ad multas multorum amicorum respondet, de suæ typographiæ statu, nominatimque de suo Thesauro Linguae Graecae. In posteriore autem eius parte, quàm misera sit hoc tempore veterum scriptorum conditio, in quorundam typographorum prela incidentium, exponit. Index Librorum qui ex officina eiusdem Henrici Stephani hactenus prodierunt. [*Geneva*], 1569, 12mo

STEPHANUS (H.). Pseudocicero . . . . . du Statu suae Typographiae et Artis Typographicæ Querimonia. *Halae*, 1737, 12mo

STEPHENSON. Life of William Caxton [*Library of Useful Knowledge*]. *London*, 184—, 8vo

STEPHENSON (S. & C.). Catalogue of the Stock in Trade . . . . which will be sold by auction by Mr. C. Heydinger. 1797, 8vo

STEPHENSON (S. & C.). Specimen of Printing Types and various Ornaments by. *London*, 1796, 8*vo*

STEPHENSON, BLAKE, & Co. Specimen of Combination Borders. New Series. *Sheffield*, 1850, 4º

STEPHENSON, BLAKE, & Co. Specimen of Printing Types. *London*, 8*vo*

STÉRÉOTYPIE PERFECTIONNÉ (La), et de son véritable Inventeur. *Paris*, 1834, 8º

STIMMEN Alsatischer Sänger beim Gutenbergs-Feste (24., 25. und 26. Juni 1840). [*Strassburg*, 1840, 8*vo*]

STÖBER (August). Die Erfindung der Buchdruckerkunst. Ein Gespräch der Elsässichen Schulejugend gewidmet. *Strassburg*, 1840, 8*vo*

STOCKMAR & WAGNER. Schatten und Licht. Eine Festgabe zur vierten Säcularfest der erfindung der Buchdruckerkunst. *Frankfort*, 1840, 4*to*

STOCKMEYER (Imm.) und REBER (Balt.). Beiträge zur Basler Buchdruckergeschichte. *Basel*, 1840, sm. 4*to*

STÖGER (Franz Xaver). Zwei der ältesten deutschen Druckdenkmäler beschrieben und in neuem Abdruck mitgelheilt. *Munchen*, 1833, 8*vo* 4 *facsimile plates*

STOUPE. Réflexions sur les Contrefaçons en Librairie; suivies d'un Mémoire sur le Rétablissement d'un Mémoire de la Communauté des Imprimeurs de Paris. *Paris an XII* (1801), 8º

STOWER (Charles). The Compositor's and Pressman's Guide to the Art of Printing. *London*, 1808, 12º

STOWER (C.). The Master Printer's Price Book; containing the Master Printer's Charges to the Trade for printing works of various sizes, types and pages. *London*, 1814, 8*vo*

STOWER (C.). The Printer's Grammar : containing a concise History of the Origin of Printing; also an examination of the superficies, gradation and properties of the different sizes of Types cast by Letter Founders . . . . . . chiefly collected from Smith's edition. To which are added Directions for Pressmen &c. The whole calculated for the Service of All who have any Concern in the Letter Press. *London*, 1787, 8º

STOWER (C.). The Printer's Grammar; or Introduction to the Art of Printing : containing a concise History of the Art, with the improvements in the practice of Printing, for the last fifty years. *London*, 1808, 8*vo*

STOWER (C.). Typographical Marks employed in correcting proofs explained and exemplified, for the use of authors. *London*, 1806, 8*vo*

STRACKERJAN (C. F.). Geschichte das Buchdruckerei in Oldenburg und Jever. *Oldenburg*, 1840, 8*vo Facsimiles*

STRAELEN (J. B. van der). Geslagt-lijste der nakomelingen van Chr. Plantin, boekdrukker binnen Antwerpen met gelagt-lijsten der familie Moretus. *Antwerpen*, 1858, 4*to Plates*

STRASBOURG. Die Erfindung der Buchdruckerkunst zu Strassburg durch Joh. Gutenberg. Kurze Notiz, herausgegeben bei Gelegenheit der vierten Säcularfeier dieser Erfindung, welche zu Strassburg den 24sten, 25sten und 26sten Juni 1840 statt hat. *Strassburg* [1840], **8vo**

STRENNA (Prima) Tipografica [*an album and almanac issued by the Italian Typographic Society*]. **Firenze**, 1871, 8*vo*

STRUTT (Joseph). A Biographical Dictionary, containing an Historical Account of all the Engravers from the earliest period of the Art of Engraving to the present time. 2 vols. *London*, 1785-6, 4°

STUCKRAD (Georg). Programm für das Gutenbergs-Jubiläum des 19n Jahrhunderts. *Offenbach*, 1837, 8*vo*

STUTTGARDT. Das vierte Säcularfest der Erfindung der Buchdruckerkunst, begangen zu Stuttgart am 24. und 25 Juni 1840. *Stuttgart*, 1840, 4*to View of the marketplace and folding plate of procession*

SULKOWSKI (J. A. M. de). Vier-honderdjarig Jubelfeest van de uitvinding der Boekdrukkunst door Laurens Janszoon Koster, gevierd te Haarlem, den 10den en 11den Julij 1823. *Amsterdam*, 1823, 8*vo*

SUSS (Maria Vinzenz). Beiträge zur Geschichte der Typographie und des Buchhandels im vormaligen Erzstifte nun Herzogthume Salzburg. *Salzburg*, 1845, 12*mo*

TABLEAU de Typographie universelle de Poche et d'Ambulance, &c. *Paris*, 1828. *Broadside, f°*

TAUBEL (Christian Gottlob). Kleines Formatbuch zum Gebrauch für Schriftsetzer. *Buchholz*, 1876, 8°

TAUBEL (C. G.). Neues theor-praktisches Lehrbuch der Buchdruckerkunst, &c. *Wien*, 1810, 8°

TAUBEL (C. G.). Orthotypographisches Handbuch; oder: Anleitung zur gründlichen Kenntniss derjenigen Theile der Buchdruckerkunst, welche allen Schriftstellern, Buchhändlern, besonders aber denen Correctoren unentbehrlich sind. Nebst einem Anhange eines typographischen Wörterbuches. *Halle*, 1785, 8*vo*

TAUBEL (C. G.). Typographisch-Technologisches Handbuch der Buchdruckerkunst für Anfänger. *Leipzig*, 1791, 8°

TAUBEL (C. G.). Wörterbuch der Buchdruckerkunst und Schriftgiesserey. *Wien*, 1805, 4*to*

TAILLANDIER (A.). Résumé historique de l'Introduction de l'Imprimerie à Paris. *Paris*, 1837, 8°

TARBÉ. Epreuves de Caractères. E. Tarbé & Cie, successeurs de Firmin Didot, Molé, Crosnier, Everat. *Paris*, 1839, 8°

TARIF pour l'Augmentation Provisoire du Prix de Main-d'œuvre d'Imprimerie. 4°

TASSIS (S. A.). Guide du Correcteur et du Compositeur. *Paris*, 1856, 12*mo*

TEISSIER (G. F.). Essai Philologique sur les Commencemens de la Typographie à Metz et sur les Imprimeurs de cette ville. *Metz*, 1828, 8*vo Portrait*

TENTZEL (Wilhelm Ernest). Discours von Erfindung der löblichen Buchdruckerkunst in Teutschland. *Gothæ*, 1700, 12°

TER BRUGGEN (Edouard). Histoire métallique et histoire de la Gravure d'Anvers, appuyées par des pièces et documents. *Anvers*, 1875, 8° Supplément. *Anvers*, 1875, 8°

TERNAUX-COMPANS (Henri). Notice sur les imprimeries qui existent ou ont existé hors de l'Europe. *Paris, no date, 8vo*

TERNAUX-COMPANS (H.). Notice sur les imprimeries qui existent ou ont existé en Europe. *Paris*, 1843, 8vo

TERNAUX-COMPANS (H.). Notice sur les imprimeries qui existent ou ont existé en Europe et hors d'Europe. Supplément. *Paris*, 1849, 8º

TERNAUX-COMPANS (H.). Nouvelles additions à la Notice sur les Imprimeries. *Paris*, 1849, 8º

TETTERODE (N.). De Tegenwoordige stand van het Lettergieters bedrijf. *Amsterdam*, 1861, 8vo

THAUSING (Moriz). Dürer, Geschichte seines Lebens und seiner kunst, mit Illustrationen. *Leipzig*, 1876, 8º

THAYER (W. M.). The Printer Boy; or how Ben Franklin made his mark. *Boston*, 1861, 12mo

THENOT (Jean Pierre). Cours complet de Lithographie. *Paris*, 1836, 4º

THIBOUST (Claude Louis). De Typographiæ Excellentiâ, Carmen. *Paris*, 1718, 8º *In Latin*

THIBOUST (C. L.). L'Excellence de l'Imprimerie. Poëme Latin, Dédié au Roi. *Paris*, 1754, 8vo

THOMAS (Isaiah). The History of Printing in America, with a Biography of Printers and an Account of Newspapers, to which is prefixed a concise view of the Discovery and Progress of the Art in other parts of the World. 2 vols. *Worcester*, 1850, 8vo

THOMAS (I.). The History of Printing in America, with a Biography of Printers and an account of Newspapers. Second edition, with the author's corrections and additions, and a Catalogue of American Publications previous to the Revolution of 1776. Published under the supervision of a special committee of the American Antiquarian Society. 2 vols. *Albany*, 1874, 8vo

THONNELIER. Notice sur les Presses Mécaniques de M. Thonnelier, bréveté d'invention et d'importation. *Paris*, 1832, 8vo

THOROWGOOD (W.). Specimen of Printing Types. *London*, 1827, 8vo

THURINGISCH-ERFURTER Gedenkbuch der vierten Säcular-Jubelfeier der Erfinding der Buchdruckerkunst zur Erfurt am 26. und 27. Juli, 1840. *Erfurt*, 1840, 8vo

TIMPERLEY (C. H.). Dictionary of Printers and Printing, Historical, Chronological, and Biographical, with the Progress of Literature, Ancient and Modern, Bibliographical Illustrations, &c. *Second Edition*. *London*, 1842, *royal 8vo*

TIMPERLEY (C. H.). The Printers' Manual; containing Instructions to Learners, with Scales of Impositions, and numerous calculations, recipes and scales of Prices in the principal towns of Great Britain: together with practical directions for conducting every department of a Printing Office. *London*, 1838, *royal 8vo*

TIMPERLEY (C. H.) Songs of the Press and other Poems relative to the Art of Printers and Printing. *London*, 1845, 12mo

TIPOGRAFIA Italiana (La) giornale professionale. 3 vols. *Firenze*, 1868-71, 4º (*All published*)

TISCHBEIN (Johann Heinrich). Die Radier-und Aetzkunst. *Zwickau*, 1827, 4º, *with 20 etchings*

TISSANDIER (Gaston). L'Héliogravure, son Histoire et ses Procédés, ses Applications à l'Imprimerie et à la Librairie. Conférence faite au Cercle de la Librairie. *Paris*, 1874, 8vo

TISSANDIER (G.). Histoire de la Gravure Typographique. Conférence faite au Cercle de la Librairie. *Paris*, 1875, *imp*. 8vo *Reprinted from the Journal Général de la Libraire*

TISSIER (Louis). Historique de la Gravure Typographique sur Pierre et le Tissiérographie. *Paris*, 1843, 8º

TODERINI (Giambattista) Letteratura Turchesca. 3 vols. *Venezia*, 1787, 8vo [*Vol. 3 treats of the history of Printing in Turkey*]

TONELLI (Francesco). Cenni storici sull' origine della Stampa e sull' artefice che primo fece uso dei caratteri sciolti e fusi. *Firenze*, 1800, 8º

TONINI (Luigi). Sulle Officine Tipografiche Riminesi, Memorie e Documenti. *Bologna*, 1866, *large 4to*

TORNABENE (Franc.). Storia critica della Tipografia Siciliana dal 1471 al 1536. *Catania*, 1839, 8º

TORY (Geoffroy). Champfleury, auquel est contenu lart et science de la deue et vraye proportiõ des lettres Attiques, quō dit autremō Lettres Antiques, et vulgairement Lettres Romaines proportionees, selon le Corps et Visage humaine. *Paris*, 1529, 4°

Tosi (Paolo Ant.). Facsimile di alcune imprese di Stampatori Italiani dei secolo XV. e XVI. *Milano*, 1838, 8°

Tosto (S.). Notizia sull' esistenza di una tipografia in Catania anteriore di anno 60 al Sinodo di M. Torres. *Catania*, 1839, 8°

Toszka (J. A.). Ueber den Satz des Polischen mit besonderer Berüchsichtigung der Theilung der Worte. Für correctoren und Setzer. *Leipzig*, 1868, 12mo

Toszka (J. A.). Ueber den Satz des Russischen. *Leipzig*, 1868, 12mo

Trattner (J. T.). Specimen Characterum . . . existentium in Typorum Fusura. *Vindobonæ*, 1760, 4to

Troyes. Illustration de l'ancienne Imprimerie Troyenne. 210 Gravures sur Bois des XVe, XVIe, XVIIe, et XVIIIe siècles. Publiés par V. L. *Troyes*, 1850, 4to *Eighty copies printed*

Trumbull (Geo.). Pocket Typographia. A brief practical Guide to the Art of Printing. *Albany*, 1846, 32mo

Tschaschlau (Waldemar de). Essai Satirique sur les vignettes, fleurons, culs-de-lampe et autres ornements des Livres. Traduction libre de l'Allemand. *Paris*, 1873, 8° *Only 200 copies printed*

Tudot (F.). Traité de Lithographie, &c. *Paris*, 1834, 18°

Turgan. Etudes sur l'Exposition Universelle, 1867. *Paris*, impl. 8° *The first 26 pages are occupied by an account of the Printing and Stationery Departments*

Turin. Regolamento della Pia Unione de' lavoranti dell' illustre arte Tipografica di Torino. *Torino*, 1825, 8vo

Turkey. Sur l'Imprimerie Turque de Constantinople. *MS. of 13 pages.* 4to, *about* 1800

Turri (Giuseppe). Memorie sull' introduzione della Stampa in Reggio d'Emilia e sua provincia nel secolo XV. *Reggio nell' Emilia*, 1869, 8vo

Twyn (John). An exact Narrative of the Tryal and Condemnation of John Twyn for Printing and Dispersing of a Treasonable Book. *London*, 1664, 4to

TYNEN (G. van) EN ZONEN. Soorten van Letteren, dewelke benevens vele andere Soorten zoo Hebreeuwsche, Grieksche, Arabische, Syrische, Hoogduitsche, Schwabacher, Latynsche als Oud-Hollandsche Geschreveue Schriften voor Boek-en Kantoorwerken, benevens allerlei Hoofdletters voor openbare aankondigingen, alsmede onderscheidene Bloemen en Vignetten. *Amsterdam*, 1832, 4*to*

TYPOGRAPHE. Eloge en vers de l'Imprimerie, par un Typographe. *Paris*, 1827, 8º

TYPOGRAPHIA, oder die Buchdruckerkunst, eine Erfindung der Deutschen; bei gelegenheit der vierten Harlemer Secularfeier zur Ehre dieser Kunst in Erinnerung gebracht. *Eisen*, 1823, 8*vo*

TYPOGRAPHIA, of betoog, dat de Boekdrukkunst eene uitvinding de Duitschers is. Uitgegeven bij gelegenheid van de viering van het vierde Eeuwfeest dier kunst, te Haarlem. *Francker*, 1823, 8*vo*

TYPOGRAPHIC ADVERTISER. Mackellar, Smiths, and Jordan, quarterly. *Philadelphia*, 1854, &c., 4*to*

TYPOGRAPHIC MESSENGER. James Conner's Sons. Quarterly. *New York*, 1866, &c. 4*to*

TYPOGRAPHICAL CIRCULAR, &c. *London*, 1854-6, 8º

TYPOGRAPHICAL HANDBOOK, The. A collection of useful information and valuable tables of interest to the Apprentice, the Book and Job Printer, the Newspaper Compositor, the Pressman, &c.; also Memoranda of important events connected with the Art. Compiled by a Practical Printer. *Detroit*, 1874, 32*mo*

TYPOLOGIE, die Lehre von Abdrücken oder van Buchstaben überhandlung. *Hamburg*, *s. a.* 8º

TYPOLOGIE-TUCKER. Notes sur la Fonderie en Caractères et sur l'Imprimerie et ses fournitures. [No. 1, May, 1874.] *Paris*, 4º (*Monthly, in progress*)

TYROL (The). Verzeichniss Typographischer Denkmäler aus dem fünfzehenten Jahrhundert. 2 vols. *Brixen*, 1789, 4*to*

CKERMANN (J. J.). Schriften Verzeichniss. *Erfurt*, 1828, 12mo

UEBERSETZUNG derjenigen Artikel der K. K. Dekrete, welche die Buchdruckerey und den Buchhandel betreffen, und einiger von dem Herrn General-Direktor gegebenen Instruktionen zu derselben Ausführung zum Gebrauch der Herren Buchhandler und Buchdrucker in den Departementen der Elb-und-Weser-Mündungen-August. 1811. 4to

UITVINDING der Boekdrukkunst. *Harlem*, 1854, 8vo

ULLMANN (Dr. C.). Rede bei dem vierten Säcularfeste der Erfindung der Buchdruckerkunst am 24sten Juni, 1840 in der akademischen Aula zu Heidelberg. *Heidelberg*, 1840, 8vo

UMBREIT (A. E.). Die erfindung der Buchdruckerkunst, kritische Abhandlungen zer Orientirung auf dem jetzigen Standpunkte der Forschung. *Leipzig*, 1843, 8vo

UNGAR (K.). Neue Beiträge zur alten Geschichte der Buchdruckerkunst in Böhmen, &c. *Prag*, 1795, 4º

UNGER (Carl). Flüchtige Blicke auf die letzten vierzig Jahre des vierten Jahrhunderts der Buchdruckerkunst. Zum Besten des bei der vierten Säcularfeier in Berlin zu gründenden Gutenberg-Fonds. *Berlin*, 1840, 8vo

UNGER (C. Th.). De Aldi Pii Manutii Romani vita meritisque in rem literatam liber Ungeri singularis auctus, cura et studio S. L. Geret. *Vitembergae*, 1753, 4to

UNGER (Johann Friedrich). Etwas über Buchhandel, Buchdruckerey, und den Druck ausserhalb Landes. *Berlin*, 1788, 4º

UNGER (J. F.). Etwas über die Holz-oder Formschneidekunst und ihren Nutzen für den Buchdrucker. *Berlin, no date*, 4º

UNION des Sentences de Philosophie. [*Specimen of cursive type.*] *Paris*, 1560, 12mo

UNUMSTOSSLICHER Beweis dass im Jahre 3,446 vor Christus am 7. September die Sündfluth geendet habe und die Alphabete aller Völker erfunden worden seien. Ein Beitrag zur Kirchengeschichte des alten Testamentes und zur vierten Säcularfeier des Typendruckes. *Leipzig*, 1840, 8*vo*

UNWIN BROTHERS. The Gresham Steam Press. Printing Types and Ornaments used by Unwin Brothers, Printers, &c. *London*, 187—, *royal* 8*vo*

URSIN (G. F.). Bogtrykkerkunstens Opfindelse og Udvikling i 400 Aar. *Kjöbenhavn*, 1840, 8*vo Only fifty copies printed*

UTRECHT. Optogt der Boekdrukkers-en Binders-Gezellen met werkende Zet-Druk-en Binderij bij gelegenheid van het tweede Eeuwfeest van de Utrechtsche Hoogeschool. *Utrecht*, 1836, 8*vo*

VADE - MECUM Typographique. *Paris*, 1866, 12*mo*

VALTUCH. Psicografia con figure analoghe, 1870, 8º

VANDERHAEGHEN (Ferdinand). Bibliographie Gantoise. Recherches sur la vie et les travaux des Imprimeurs de Gand (1483-1850). 7 vols. *Gand*, 1858-67, 8*vo*

VAN WINKLE (C. S.). The Printers' Guide; or, an Introduction to the Art of Printing: including an essay on Punctuation, and Remarks on Orthography. *New York*, 1818, 12*mo*

VARUSOLTIS. Xylographie de l'Imprimerie Troyenne pendant le XVe-XVIIIe siècle. *Troyes*, 1859, 4*to*

VEEN (B. W. Van der). De Verbeterde Nederlandsche Letterkast. *Tiel*, 1852, 8*vo*

VERGIL. Polydori Vergilii Urbinatis, de Rerum Inventoribus, Libri viii. et de Prodigiis, Libri iii. cum Indicibus, Locupletissimis. *Lugd.-Batavorum,* 1644, 12*mo Chapter vii. of the 2nd book treats of Books, Libraries, and the Invention of Printing, which is attributed to Gutenberg at Mayence. The engraved title-page bears a full-length figure of Gutenberg, with the Inscription, "Typographiæ Inventor"*

VERMIGLIOLI (G. B.). Lettera sulla Tipografia Perugina del Secolo XV. *Perugia*, 1806, 8º

VERMIGLIOLI (G. B.). Principi della Stampa in Perugia e suoi progressi per tutto il secolo XV. *Perugia*, 1820, 8vo

VERNAZZA (Giuseppe). Dizionario dei Tipografi e dei principali Correttori ed Intagliatori che operarono negli Stati Sardi e piu specialmente in Piemonte sino all' anno 1821. *Torino*, 1859, 4º

VERNAZZA (G.). Lezione sopra de la Stampa. *Cagliari*, 1778, 12mo

—— Appendice del medesimo alla Lezione, &c *Torino*, 1787, 8vo

VERNAZZA (G.). Osservazione sopra gli Annali Tipografici del Panzer. *Torino*, 1793, 8vo

VERNAZZA (G.). Osservazioni tipografiche sopra libri impressi in Piemonte nel secolo XV. *Bassano*, 1807, 8vo

VERNAZZA (G.). Della Tipografia in Alba nel secolo XV. *Torino*, 1815, 8vo

VERNAZZA (G.). Della tipografia de' Torrentini in Mondovi. *Firenze*, 1813, 8vo

VERTUE (George). A Catalogue of Engravers who have been born, or resided, in England; digested by Horace Walpole, Earl of Orford, from the MSS. of Mr. George Vertue; to which is added an account of the life and works of the latter. *London*, 1794, 8vo *Portraits*

VERZEICHNISS einiger in der akademischen Aula am 25. und 26. Juni, 1840, zur Ansicht aufgestellter in der hiesigen Universitätsbibliothek aufbewahrter alter Druckwerke. *Leipzic*, 1840, 8vo

VESTER (Christian). Löbliche Buchdruckerkunst, nach dero ursprünglichen, &c. *Halle* [1660], 4º

VIENNA. Beurtheilungen über die K. K. Hof-und Staatsdruckerei in Wien. *Wien*, 1852, 8vo

VIENNA. Specimens of Chromo-Lithography, &c. Executed at the Imperial Printing Establishment at Vienna, as exhibited at the Great Exhibition of 1851. *Impl. folio*, 1851, 70 *plates*

VIENNA. Specimens of Typography, executed at the Imperial Establishment at Vienna, consisting of Facsimiles of Manuscripts from the Sixth Century to the Invention of Printing. The type of the Gutenberg Bible, Ornamental Letters, Foreign

Characters, &c., as exhibited at the Great Exhibition of 1851. *Impl. fol*, 1851

VIETOR (J. L.). Neu-aufgesetztes Format Buchlein. Ubersehen, &c., von J. Redinger. *Frankf.-a-M.*, 1679, 8º

VILLARROYA (Joseph). Disertacion sobre el origen del nobilisimo Arte Tipografico y su Introduccion y uso en la Ciudad de Valencia de los Edetanos. *Valencia*, 1796, 8vo

VINCARD (B.). L'Art du Typographe contenant les détails de chacun des deux parties de cette Science, &c. [*List of contents follows.*] *Paris*, 1806, 8vo— *Paris*, 1823, 8vo

VINCARD (B.). Idée sur l'origine de l'Imprimerie, ses progrès jusqu'à ce jour; et la perfection dont elle est encore susceptible. *Paris n. d.*, 8º

VINCENT (J. B.). Essai sur l'Histoire de l'Imprimerie en Belgique, depuis le XVᵉ jusqu'à la fin du XVIIIᵉ Siècle. *Bruxelles*, 1859, 8vo *Fifty copies only printed from the "Bulletin du Bibliophile Belge,"* vol. xv.

VINCENT (J. B.). Essai sur l'Histoire de l'Imprimerie en Belgique, depuis le XVᵐᵉ jusqu'à la fin du XVIIIᵐᵉ Siècle. *Bruxelles*, 1867, 8vo *350 copies printed*

VÖGELIN (S.). Christ. Froschaver, erster berühmter Buchdrucker in Zürich, nach seinem Leben und Wirken. *Zurich*, 1840, 4to

VOISIN (A.). Notes pour servir à l'Histoire de l'Imprimerie dans l'Ancienne Belgique. [*Bruxelles*, 1850], 8vo *Reprinted from the "Bulletin de l'Académie Royale de Bruxelles," vol. v., No. 10*

VOISIN (A.). Sur quelques imprimeries particulières des Pays-Bas. 2e éd. *Gand*, 1840, 8º

VOISIN (A.). J. Lambert . . . imprimeur et graveur gantois du 16ᵉ siècle. (*Gand* c. 1845), 8º

VOLGER (E.). Die Correctur wie sie gelesen werden muss. *München*, 1835, 8º

VOLPI (Gaetano). La libreria de' Volpi, e la stamperia Cominiana. Illustrate con utili e curiose Annotazioni Avvertenze necessarie e profittevoli a' Bibliothecarj e agli Amatori de' buoni Libri. *Padova*, 1756, sm. 8vo (*Only 200 copies printed*)

VOLTA (L. C.). Saggio Storico-critico sulla tipografia Mantovana del secolo XV. *Venezia*, 1786, 4º

VRIES (A. de). Bewijsgronden der Duitschers voor hunne aanspraak op de uitvinding der Boekdrukkunst, of beoordeeling van het werk van A. E. Umbreit: Die Erfindung der Buchdruckerkunst. 'sGravenhage, 1844, 8vo

VRIES (A. de). Arguments des Allemands en faveur de leur prétention à l'Invention de l'Imprimerie, ou examen critique de l'ouvrage de M. A. E. Umbreit: Die Erfindung der Buchdruckerkunst. Traduit du hollandais par J. J. F. Noordziek. La Haye, 1845, royal 8vo

VRIES (A. de). Bijdragen tot de Geschiedenis der Uitvinding van de Boekdrukkunst. Haarlem, 1823, 8vo Privately printed

VRIES (A. de). Eclaircissements sur l'histoire de l'invention de l'Imprimerie contenant: Lettre à M. A. D. Schinkel, ou Réponse à la notice de M. Guichard sur le Speculum Humanæ Salvationis; Dissertation sur le nom de Coster et sur sa prétendu charge de sacristain; Recherches faites à l'occasion de la quatrième fête séculaire à Haarlem en 1823 . . . traduit du hollandais par J. J. F. Nordzeik. La Haye, 1843, royal 8vo

VRIES (A. de). Brief aan A. D. Schinkel over Guichard's Notice sur le Speculum Humanæ Salvationis, met drie Bijlagen tot staving der naauwkeurigheid van het verhaal van Junius wegens de Uitvinding der Boekdrukkunst enter wederlegging der meening: Dat Coster koster zou geweest zijn. 'sGravenhage, 1841, 8vo

VRIES (A. de). Lijst des stukken betr. de geschiedenis der boekdrukkunst op het Stadhuis te Haarlem. Haarlem, 1862, 8vo

WALDAU (G. E.). Leben Ant. Koburger, einen der erster und berühmtesten Buchdrucker in Nürnberg, &c. Dresden and Leipzig, 1786, 8º

WALDHECKER. Die Kunst einen gleichförmigen Druck bei Steindruck zu erreichen. Osnabrück, 1832, 8º

WALDOW (Alexander). Die Buchdruckerkunst uber die verwandten Geschäftszweig. *Leipzig*, 1871, 4to

WALDOW (A.). Hülfs-Buchlein für Buchdrucker und Schriftsetzer sowie für Factoren, Correctoren und Verlagsbuchhändler. *Leipzig*, 1872, 12mo

WALDOW (A.). Kurzer Rathgeber für die Behandlung der Farben. *Leipzig*, 1868, 12mo

WALDOW (A.). Taschen-Agenda für Buchdrucker-Schreib-Merk-und Notiz-Kalender. *Leipzig*, 1876, 8vo

WALTER (J.). An Address to the Public by J. Walter, showing the great improvement he has made in the art of printing, by Logographic arrangements, &c. *London*, 1789, 8º

WALTHER. Catalogue Méthodique des dissertations ou thèses académiques imprimées par les Elzevir de 1616-1712. Supplément aux Annales de l'Imprimerie des Elzevirs publiée par M. Ch. Pieters à Gand. *Bruxelles*, 1864, 8º

WATSON (James). The History of the Art of Printing, with a Preface to the Printers in Scotland [by John Spottiswoode]. *Edinburgh*, 1713, 8vo

WATT (P. B.). A few hints on Colour and Printing in Colours. *London*, 1872, 12mo

WEGELIN (P.). Die Buchdruckereien der Schweiz, mit erläuternden und ergänzenden Anmerkungen. Eine Gelegenheitschrift zur Feier des vierten Jubelfestes der Erfindung der Buchdruckerkunst. *St. Gallen*, 1836, 12mo

WEGELIN (P.). Geschichte der Buchdruckereien in Kanton St. Gallen. Mit einleitender nachricht über die erfindung der Buchdruckerkunst. Eine Festgabe für die Theilnehmer an der Säkularfeier in St. Gallen am 24. Juni, 1840. *St. Gallen*, [1840], 12mo

WEIGEL (T. O.). Catalogue des Premières productions de l'art d'Imprimer. *Leipzig*, 1872, 8vo

WEIGEL (T. O.) und ZESTERMANN (Ad.). Die Anfänge der Druckerkunst in bild und schrift an deren frühesten Erzeugnissen in der Weigl'schen Sammlung erläutert. 2 vols. *Leipzig*, 1866, *folio, facsimiles*

WEIMAR's Album zur IVn Säcularfeier der Buchdruckerkunst. *Weimar*, 1840, 8vo

WEISHAUPT (Heinrich). Das Gesammtgebiet des Steindrucks oder vollständige theoretisch-praktische Anweisung zur Ausübung der Lithographie in ihrem ganzen Umfange und auf ihrem jetzigen Standpunkte. Nebst einem Anhange von der Zinkographie, dem anastatischen Drucke, und der Photolithographie. Nebst einem Atlas von 12 Tafeln, enthaltend 140 Abbildungen. *Weimar*, 1875, *crown* 8º *Atlas*, 12 *plates, oblong* 8*vo*

WEISHAUPT (H.). Theoretisch-Praktische Anleitung zur Chromo-Lithographie. *Quedlinburg*, 1848, 8º

WELDAAD der Boekdrukkunst (De) voor het menschelijke geslacht, dankbaar herdacht bij de onthulling van het metalen standbeeld ter eere van Lourens Janszoon Coster, te Haarlem, den 16en Julij 1856. *'sGravenhage*, 1857, 8*vo*

WELLER (E.). Repertorium typographicum. Die deutsche Literatur im ersten Viertel des 16ten Jahrhunderts. *Nördlingen*, 1868, 8*vo*

WESTERMAN (M.). Aan de Feestvierende Drukkers-Gezellen, van de Heeren Blussé & Comp. en J. de Vos & Comp., te Dordrecht, den 10 Julij 1823, 8*vo*

WESTREENEN VAN TIELLANDT (W. H. J.). Bewijzen voor de Echtheid en gelijkenis der oude afbeeldingen van Coster. *Haarlem*, 1847, 8*vo*

WESTREENEN. De Zoogenaamde "Bewijzen voor de Echtheid, &c.," wederlegd door den Baron W. v. T. *'sGravenhage*, 1848, 4*to*

WESTREENEN. Iets over de afbeeldingen van Laurens Jansz. Koster. *Gravenhage*, 1847, 12*mo*

WESTREENEN. Korte Schets van den voortgang de Boekdrukkunst in Nederland in de XVde. en haare verdere volmaaking in XVIde. en de XVIIde. eeuw. *'sGravenhage*, 1829, 8*vo*

WESTREENEN. Rapport sur les Recherches relatives à l'Invention première et à l'usage le plus ancien de l'Imprimerie Stéréotype faites à la demande du Gouvernement. [*In French and German.*] *La Haye*, 1833, 8*vo*

WESTREENEN. Verhandeling over de Uitvinding der Boekdrukkunst; in Holland oorspronkelijk uitgedacht, te Straatsburg verbeterd en te Mentz voltooid. *'sHage*, 1809, 8*vo*

WETTER (Johann). Beantwortung der Frage: in welchem Jahre ist die Buchdruckerkunst erfunden worden? *Mainz*, 1837, 8°

WETTER (J.). Conrad Henlif oder Henekis, Buchdrucker und Buchhandler zu Mainz, der Geschafftsgenosse Peter Schöffer's. *Mainz*, 1851, 8vo

WETTER (J.). Kritische Geschichte der Erfindung der Buchdruckerkunst durch Johann Gutenberg zu Mainz; mit einer neuen Untersuchung der Ansprüche der Stadt Harlem. *Mainz, 1836, 8vo, and folio Atlas of 13 plates*

WHO was the first Printer? In "St. Paul's," No. 12. *London*, September, 1868, 8°

WICHTIGSTE (Das) der Buchdruckerkunst, &c. *Leipzig*, 1838, f°

WIEBEKING (C. F.). Ueber Typographische Carten. *Mülheim*, 1792, 4to

WIECHMANN-KADOW (C. M.). Beiträge zur ältern Buchdruckergeschichte Mecklenburgs, nebst einer Zusammenstellung der bisher beschriebenen Meklenburgischen Druckdenkmale. *Schwerin*, 1857, 8vo

WIECHMANN-KADOW (C. M.). Die Mecklenburgischen Formschneider des XVI. Jahrhunderts. *Schwerin*, 1858, 8vo

WILLEMS (J. F.). Berigten wegens de Boekprinters van Antwerpen, 1442, &c. *Gent*, 1844, 8vo

WILLEMS (J. F.). Bijdrage tot de geschiedenij der Boekdrukkunst in Antwerpen, &c. *Antwerpen*, 1828, 8°

WILLETT (Ralph). A Memoir on the Origin of Printing. Article in the "Archæologia," vol. XI., pp. 267-316. *London*, 4to

WILLETT (Ralph). Observations on the Origin of Printing. Article in the "Archæologia," vol. VIII., pp. 239-250. *London*, 1787, 4to

WILLETT (Ralph). A Memoir of the Origin of Printing. In a letter addressed to John Topham, Esq. *Newcastle*, 1820, 8vo *Reprinted from "Archæologia." 150 copies printed, of which 30 were on large paper*

WILLSHIRE (William Hughes). An Introduction to the Study and Collection of Ancient Prints. Second edition, revised and enlarged. 2 vols. *London*, 1877, 8vo

WILME (B. P.). A **Manual** of Writing and Printing Characters, both ancient and modern, for the use of architects, engineers, and surveyors, engravers, **printers,** decorators, and draughtsmen; also **for** use in schools and private families; in which **the** various alphabets in everyday use **are** completely analyzed and familiarly explained; containing numerous examples of curious ancient alphabets. Illustrated with 26 large plates and **17** woodcuts. *London, published for the author*, 1845, **4to**

WILSON (Alexander) and Sons. A Specimen of Printing Types **cast in the Letter** Foundry of. *Glasgow*, 1786, **8vo**

WILSON (A. J.). The **Walter Press** [*article in* "*Macmillan's Magazine*," **Feb.** 1875], *8vo*

WILSON (John). A Treatise on English Punctuation; designed **for** Letter Writers, Printers **and** Correctors of the **Press,** and for the use of Schools and Academies. With an Appendix containing rules on the Use of Capitals, a List of Abbreviations, Hints **on** the Preparation of Copy and on Proof Reading, Specimens of Proof **Sheets,** &c. *Boston*, 1850, 16*mo*

WILSON (J. S.). Autotypie. **De Natuur zich zelve** afbeeldende. *Meppel*, 1857, *oblong*

WINARICKY (Charles). Jean Gutenberg, né en 1412, à Kuttenberg en Bohême, Bachelier des Arts à l'Université de Prague, promu le 18 Novembre, 1445, inventeur de l'Imprimerie à Mayence, 1450. Essai Historique et Critique. Traduit du Manuscrit Allemand par le Jean Chevalier de Carro. *Bruxelles*, 1847, 12*mo*

WITTIG (C. F.) and FISCHER (C. F.). Die Schnellpresse, &c. *Leipzig*, 1861, 8°

WOLF (Joh. Christian). Monumenta typographica, quæ artis hujus præstantissimæ originem, laudem et abusum posteris produnt. 2 vols. *Hamburgi*, 1740, *small 8vo*

> The following **treatises are** reprinted in these two thick **volumes**:—
>
> Bergellani (Jo. Arn.) Poëma de Chalcographiæ inventione
> Stephani (Henr.) Artis typographicæ querimonia, & Epitaphia Typographorum **doctorum**
> Judicis (Matth.) Libellus de typographiæ inventione & de prælorum inspectione

Besoldi (Christoph.) Dissert. de inventione Typographiæ

Scriverii (Pet.) Laurea Laurentii Costeri, è belgico

Anonymi (Fausti) Relatio MS. de Origine Typographiæ, è germanico

Ex Naudaei (Gabr.) Additamentis ad Historiam Ludovici XI. Regis Galliarum, è gallico

Ex Boxhornii (Marci Zuerii) Theatro urbium Hollandiæ

Mallincrot (Bernh.) Dissert. de ortu et progressu artis typographicæ

Boxhornii (Marci Zuerii) Dissert. de typographicæ artis inventione

Ex ejusdem Historia Universali

Rivini (Andr.) Hecatomba laudum ob inventam Chalcographiam

Ejusdem Oratio de artis Typographicæ præstantia

Brehmen (C.) Expositio inventionis artis typographicæ cum carminibus latinis variorum, è germanico

Carmina Secularia de Typographia, cura G. Baumanni excusa

Kleinvvechters (Valent.) Actus Seculares II. in laudem typographiæ

Starckii (Sebast. Gottfr.) Oratio de arte typographica, è germanico

Rivini (Andr.) Controversiæ de artis typographicæ inventione, è germanico

Gveintzii (Christiani) Encomium artis typographicæ, è germanico

Insulani Menapii (Gulielmi) Statera Chalcographiæ

Schragii (J. Adami) Historia Typographiæ, è germanico

Schmidii (Jo.) Conciones III. Eucharisticæ, è germanico

Boecleri (Jo. Henr.) Oratio de Typographiæ divinitate

Mentelii (Jac.) Brevis excursus de loco, tempore et autore inventionis Typographiæ, cum notis MSS.

Ejusdem Parænesis de Typographiæ origine

Ejusdem Observationes MSS. de Typographis & Typographia

Gutneri (Jo. Gabr.) Typographiæ Chemnitiensis primæ plagulæ, è germanico

Fritschii (Ahasv.) Dissert. de abusibus Typographiæ tollendis

Stobrii (Jo.) Dissert. de ortu Typographiæ
Vesteri (Christiani) Nobilissima ars typographica descripta, è germanico
Fritschii (Ahasv.) Dissert. de Typographis
Normanni (Laur.) Dissert. de Typographia
Licimandri Panegyricus in laudem artis typographicæ, è germanico
Mollers (Dan Guilh.) Dissert. de Typographia
Schroedteri (Ern. Christiani) Dissert. de Typographia
Thiboust (C. Ludov.) Carmen Latinum
Tentzelii (Wilh. Ern.) Diss. de inventione Typographicæ, è germanico
Krausii (Jo. Christoph.) **Laudes Typographiæ**, è germanico
Petris (Pauli) Dissert. de Typis Literarum
Fekno (Pet. Pauli) Programme de typographia et pulvere pyrio
Oudini (Casim.) Dissert. de primis artis typographicæ inventoribus
Tolandi (Jo.) Conjectura de Typographiæ inventione
Natolini (J. Bap.) Diss. de arte imprimendi, ex italico
Catherinot (Nic.) Ars imprimendi, è Gallico
Bockenhofferi (Jo. Phil.) Brevis relatio, è danico
Observationes de ortu et progressu Typographiæ, ex anglico
Bagfordi (Jo.) Exercitatio de inventione Typographiæ, ex anglico
Loca selecta & carmina variorum

Wood and Sharwoods. The Specimen Book of Types cast at the Austin Letter Foundry. *London*, 1839, 4º; 1844, 4º

Wurdtwein (S. A.). Bibliotheca Moguntina, libris sæculo primo typographiæ Moguntinæ impressis instructa; hinc inde addita Inventæ Typographiæ Historia. *Augustæ Vindelicorum*, 1789, 4to

YOUNG and MINNS. The Defence of Young and Minns, Printers to the State, before the Committee of the House of Representatives. With an Appendix containing the Debate. *Boston*, 1805, 8vo

ZACCARIA ANTONUCCI (Gaetano). Catalogo ragionato di opere stampate per Francesco Marcolini da Forlî, con memorie biografiche raccolte da Raffaele De-Minicis. *Fermo*, 1850, 8vo

ZACCARIA ANTONUCCI (G.). Catalogo di opere Ebraiche, Greche, Latine ed Italiane stampate dai celebri tipografi Soncini ne' Secoli XV e XVI ora per cura di C. Giannini corretto e migliorato, come nella prima edizione ci sono premesse le brevi Notizie storiche degli stessi Tipografi dettate dall' egregio letterato Cav. Zefirino re Cesenate. *Fermo*, 1868, 8vo *Only 250 copies printed*

ZANI (Pietro). Materiali per servire alla Storia dell' Origine e de' progressi dell' Incisione in rame, e in legno, e sposizione dell' interessante scoperta d'una stampa originale del celebre Maso Finiguerra fatta nel Gabinetto Nazionale de Parigi. *Parma*, 1802, 8°

ZANTEDESCHI (Francesco). Della Elettrotipia. *Venezia*, 1841, 4°

ZAPF (Georg Wilhelm). Aelteste Buchdruckergeschichte von Mainz, von derselben Erfindung bis 1499. *Ulm*, 1790, 8vo

ZAPF (G. W.). Aelteste Buchdruckergeschichte Schwabens. Oder Verzeichniss aller von Erfindung der Buchdruckerkunst bis 1500 in Ulm, Esslingen,

Reutlingen, Memmingen, Stuttgart, Tübingen, Urach, Blaubeuren und Costanz gedrukten Bücher, mit litterarischen Anmerkungen. *Ulm,* 1791, 8*vo*

ZAPF (G. W.). Annales Typographiæ Augustanæ ab ejus origine 1466 usque ad annum 1530; accedit F. A. Veith. Diatribe de Origine et Incrementis artis Typographicæ in urbe Augusta Vindelicâ. *Augustæ Vindelicorum,* 1778, 4*to*

ZAPF (G. W.). Buchdrucker-Geschichte Augsburgs von 1468-1530. 2 vols. *Augsburg,* 1786-91, 4*to*

ZAPF (G. W.). Ueber eine alte und höchst seltene Ausgabe von des Joannis de Turrecremata Explanatio in Psalterium und einige andere typographische Seltenheiten: eine litterarisch - bibliographische Abhandlung. *Nürnberg,* 1803, 4*to*

ZAPF (G. W.). Vorlaufige Nachricht von der ehemaligen berühmten Privatbuchdruckerey ad insigne Pinus in Augsburg. *Augsburg,* 1804, 8*vo*

ZEGGELEN (W. J. van). Costerliedjes. Souvenir aan Haarlem Julij feesten in 1856. *Haarlem,* 1856, 12*mo*

ZEISKE (J. G.). Von dem Nutzen und denen Verdiensten der Buchdruckerkunst. *Budissin,* 1740, 4º

ZELTNER (Gustav Georg). Kurtz-gefasste Historie der gedruckten Bibel-Version und anderer schriften D. Mart. Lutheri, in der Beschreibung des Lebens und Fatorum Hanns Luffts, berühmten Buchdruckers und Händlers zu Wittenberg, auch anderer dasigen und benachbarten Typographorum. *Nurnberg,* 1727, 4*to Portraits of Luffts, Rhauens, Guttenberg, Faust,* **Mentel,** *and Koster*

ZELTNER (J. C.). Correctorum in Typographiis eruditorum centuria, speciminis loco collecta. *Norimbergæ,* 1716, 8*vo*

ZELTNER (J. C.). Theatrum Virorum Eruditorum qui speciatim typographiis laudabilem operam praestiterunt. *Norimbergæ,* 1720, 12*mo*

ZENGER (John Peter). The Case and Tryal of John Peter Zenger, of New York, Printer, who was lately tryed and acquitted for Printing and Publishing a Libel against the Government, with the Pleadings and Arguments on both sides. *London,* 1750, 8*vo*

ZENO (Apostolo). Notizie letterarie intorno ai

Manuzi Stampatori, ed alla loro famiglia. *Venezia*, 1736, 8°

ZIJLL (W. C. van). Mijmering van het oude standbeeld van Laurens Janszoon Coster. (Afgeluisterd.) Ten voordeele van het feest der onthulling van diens standbeeld. *Hilversum*, 1856, 8vo

SUPPLEMENT.

BOUT (Edmond). La Justice et la Liberté dans l'Industrie Typographique. *Paris*, 1865, 12*mo*

ADELINE (Jules). L.-H. Brevière, dessinateur et graveur, rénovateur de la Gravure sur bois en France, 1797-1869. Notes sur la vie et les œuvres d'un artiste Normand. *Rouen*, 1876, 8*vo*
Portrait and six other plates. Only 125 copies printed

ANDRESEN (Andreas). Handbuch für Kupferstichsammler, oder Lexikon der Kupferstecher, Maler-Radirer und Formschneider. 2 vols. *Leipzig*, 1870-73, 8°

AROLSEN. Reden am Gutenbergsfeste zu Arolsen. 24. Juni 1840. *Arolsen*, 1840, 8*vo*

BAEDEKER (Eduard und Julius). Familien-und Geschäfts-Nachrichten, bei der Einweihung des Druckerei-Neubaues den Geschwistern in's Gedächtniss zurückgerufen. *Essen*, 1851, 12*mo*

BAGELAAR (E. W. J.). Verhandeling over eene nieuwe manier om Prenteeckeningen. *Harlem*, 1817, 8°

BASAN (Pierre François). Dictionnaire des Graveurs anciens et modernes. Seconde édition. 2 vols. *Paris*, 1789, 8° *Plates*

BASLE. XVIII. Neujahrs-Blatt für Basels Jugend herausgegeben von der Gesellschaft zu Beförderung des Guten und Gemeinnützigen 1840 [Die ersten Buckdrucker in Basel]. *Basel*, 1840, 4*to*

BERLIN. Die öffentliche Feier des vierten Säcular-Festes der Erfindung der Buchdruckerkunst in Berlin am 25. und 26. September 1840. *Berlin*, 1841, 8*vo*

BERNARD. Presse Typographique, nouveau système, bréveté, sans garantie du Gouvernement, de M. Bernard aîné, imprimeur à Montbrison. *Montbrison* [1856], 4to, pp. 3, *with two woodcuts*

BODONI. La Prefazione al Manuale Tipografico di Giambattista Bodoni, seguìta da una Dissertazione estetica di Giuseppe Chiantore, edite per cura di Salvadore Landi. *Firenze*, 1874, 8vo

BOECKEL (E. G. A.). Die Buchdruckerkunst und die Kirchenverbesserung. Predigt, am Reformationsfeste 1840. *Oldenburg* [1840], 12mo

BOEDEKER (Hermann Wilhelm). Die Geschichte und hohe Bedeutsamkeit der Buchdruckerkunst. Auf Anlass der vierten Säcularfeier ihrer Erfindung für die Hannoverschen Volkschulen. *Hannover*, 1840, 12mo

BRADBURY (Henry). Specimens of Bank Note Engraving, &c. Printed for private circulation. *London*, 1860, 4to At the end *Specimens of Bank Note Paper*, by T. H. Saunders

BROCKHAUS (F. A.) in Leipzig. Buchhandlung, Buchdruckerei, Schriftgiesserei, Stereotypengiesserei, Stahl-und Kupferdruckerei, Maschinenwerkstatt. 4to

BRUN (M.). Kurzes Practisches Handbuch der Buchdruckerkunst in Frankreich. Aus dem Französischen des M. Brun, übersetzt, und mit Züsatzen, Anmerkungen, und Zeichnungen begleitet von W. Hasper. *Carlsruhe*, 1828, 12mo

BURCKHARDT und HAGENBACH. Festreden bei der vierten Säcularfeier der Erfindung der Buchdruckerkunst in Basel gahalten im Münster daselbst von den Herren Antistes Burckhardt und Professor Hagenbach den 24sten Juni, 1840. Nebst einer Beschreibung des Festes. *Basel* [1840], 4to

CAROVÉ (Friedrich Wilhelm). Die Buchdruckerkunst in ihrer weltgeschichtlichen Bedeutung. *Siegen und Wiesbaden*, 1843, sm. 8vo

CASLON. Specimens of the ancient Caslon Printing Types engraved in the early part of last century by William Caslon, 1716, comprising:—a complete series of Roman and Italic, Blacks, Greeks, Hebrews, Saxon, Anglo-Saxon, Gothic, Coptic, Ethiopic, Armenian, Arabic, Syriac, Etruscan, Persian, Russian, &c. [*London*, 1870], *impl.* 8vo

CHOFFARD (P. P.). Notice historique sur l'art de la Gravure en France. *Paris*, 1804, 8º

CLAROMONTIUS (Gothofredus). In Statuam Laureatam quam Collegium Medicum sub auspiciis amplissimorum consulum civitatis Harlemensis Laurentio Costero viro consulari Typographiæ inventori primo in horto medico Harlemensi erexit MDCCXXIII. *Amstelædami* [1723], *folio A Latin poem of 18 lines on one page with the above title*

COBURG. Vollständige Beschreibung und Sammlung alles dessen, was bey dem den 29ten Junii, 1740, zu Coburg, auf gnädigst erhaltene Erlaubniss der Durchl. Landes-Herrschafften, wegen der vor dreyhundert Jahren erfundenen edlen Buchdrucker-Kunst gefeierten Jubilaeo vorgefallen und abgehandelt worden. *Coburg*, 1740, 12mo

DAVY (Reverend William). A System of Divinity, in a course of Sermons, &c. 26 vols. *Lustleigh, Devon. Printed by himself. Fourteen copies only.* 1795, 8vo

DELITZSCH (Franz). Der Flügel des Engels. Eine Stimme aus der Wüste im vierten Jubel-Fest-Jahre der Buchdruckerkunst. *Dresden*, 1840, 8vo

DELPIT (Jules). Origines de l'Imprimerie en Guyenne. *Bordeaux*, 1869, 8vo

DEMBOUR (A.). Description d'un nouveau procédé de Gravure en relief sur cuivre, dite Ectypographie Métallique. *Metz*, 1835, 4to

DEMBOUR (A.). Die Metall-Ektypographie. Beschreibung eines neuen Verfahrens erhaben auf Kupfer zu ätzen, erfunden von A. Dembour. Aus dem Französischen von H. Meyer. *Braunschweig*, 1835, 8vo

DENNHARDT (Professor). Anhang zur Beschreibung des Gutenbergesfestes in Erfurt. Festrede, am 27. Juli 1840. [*Erfurt*], 1840, 8vo

DIEGERICK (Alphonse). Essai de Bibliographie Yproise. Etude sur les Imprimeurs Yprois du XVIe Siècle. *Ypres*, 1873, 8vo

DIEGERICK (Alphonse). Essai de Bibliographie Yproise. Etude sur les Imprimeurs Yprois, XVIIe Siècle. *Ypres*, 1876, 8vo

DLABACZ (Gottfried Joh.). Abhandlung von den Schicksalen der Kunste in Böhmen [pp. 107-160 of "Neuern Abhandlungen der K. Böhmische Gesellschaft," vol. 3]. *Prag*, 1797, 4to

DLABACZ (G. J.). Kurzgefasste Nachricht von der noch unbekannten Buckdruckerey zu Altenberg in Böhmen. *Prag*, 1797, 4to

DRESDEN. Der löblichen Buchdrucker-Gesellschafft zu Dresden Jubel-Geschichte, Anno 1740 den 24. und 25. Junii. Mit einer Vorrede Herrn Christian Schöttgens. *Dressden* [1740], 4to

DUPONT (Paul). 1862. Exposition Universelle de Londres. Notice sur l'Etablissement Typographique de M. Paul Dupont de Paris. *Paris*, 1862, 8vo

DUPONT. Imprimerie Paul Dupont. Compte rendu de l'Assemblée Générale des Ouvriers du 14 Mai, 1863. *Paris*, 1863, 8vo

DUPONT. Imprimerie Paul Dupont. Compte rendu de l'Assemblée Générale des Ouvriers du 4 Juin, 1865. *Paris*, 1865, 8vo

DUPONT. Rapport fait à M. Paul Dupont sur la création de la Villa Typographique au Moyen d'une Société co-opérative immobilière. [*Paris*, 1868], 12mo

DUPONT. Pp. 289-320 of vol. iv. of Turgan, Les Grandes Usines. *Paris*, 1864, 8vo *Being an illustrated description of the* "*Imprimerie Administrative de M. Paul Dupont*"

EDEL (Friedrich Wilhelm). Denkschrift für die im Jahre 1840 zu begehende vierte Säcularfeier der Erfindung der Buchdruckerkunst. *Strassburg*, 1840, 12mo

ELECTRO-PRINTING BLOCK COMPANY. *Specimens of their productions in enlarging and reducing engravings, maps, music, &c. Mounted in two vols., oblong folio*

EMERSON (William A.). Practical Instruction in the art of wood engraving for persons wishing to learn the art without an instructor. Containing a description of tools and apparatus used, and explaining the manner of engraving various classes of work. Also a History of the Art from its origin to the present time. Illustrated. *East Douglas* [*Massachusetts*], 1876, 12mo

ENSCHEDÉ. Aan de wel-edele heeren Johannes Enschedé en Zoonen, bij de viering van bet onder hun ed. vijf-en-zeventig jarig bestaan der alom vermaarde Lettergieterij. [*Haarlem*], 1743, 8vo

ENSCHEDÉ. Plichtbetuiging bij gelegenheid van het huwelijk van een onzer veelgeachte meesters den heere Abraham Enschedé en mejuffrouwe Sandrina Christiana Swaving. [*Haarlem*], 1725. *A folio broadside*

ENSCHEDÉ. Plichtbetuiging bij gelegenheid van het huwelijk van den heere Jacobus Enschedé en mejuffrouwe Johanna Christina Abbensets. [*Haarlem*], 1806, 4*to*

ENSCHEDÉ. Proeve van letteren, welke gegoten worden in de Haarlemsche Lettergietery van Joh. Enschedé en Zonen. *Haarlem*, 1825, *folio*

ENSCHEDÉ. Ter Bruilofte van den heere Mr. Johannes Enschedé en mejuforowe Catherina Hillegonda van Walré. [*Haarlem*], 1810, 4*to*

ENSCHEDÉ. Ter Zilveren Bruiloft van den heere Mr. Johannes Enschedé en mevrouwe zijne echtgenoote Catherina Hillegonda van Walré. [*Haarlem*], 1835, 4*to*

FIVE BLACK ARTS: Printing, Pottery, Gas-light, Glass, Iron. *Columbus (Ohio)*, 1861, 12*mo*

FOSTER and WINSTONE. Specimens of Printing Inks, Machine, Letterpress and Lithographic. *London*, 1851, 8*vo*

FOURGEAUD-LAGRÈZE (N.). La Périgord littéraire. L'Imprimerie en Périgord, ses Origines, ses progrès et ses principales productions (1498-1874). *Ribérac*, 1876, 8*vo*

GAMBA (Bartolommeo). Biografia dell' illustre tipografo Giambattista Bodoni. [*Venezia*, 1835], 8*vo* Extract from the "*Biografia degl' Italiani Illustri del Secolo XVIII.*"

GAULLIER (Ernest). L'Imprimerie à Bordeaux en 1486. *Bordeaux*, 1869, 8°

GESCHICHTLICHE Uebersicht der Kupferstecherkunst. 3 parts. *Leipzig*, 1841, 8°

GIOVANNI (Azeglio). Relazione sul Congresso Tipografico di Feltre, letta in assemblea generale della Società dei Compositori-Tipografi di Firenze. *Firenze*, 1869, 8*vo*

GOULD (Joseph). The Letter Press Printer: a complete guide to the art of printing; containing practical instructions for learners at case, press and machine. Embracing the whole practice of book work, with diagram and complete schemes of imposition; job work, with examples; news work, colour work, to make coloured inks, to work press and machine, to make rollers, and other valuable information. *London*, 1876, 16º

GRAPHIC Portfolio (The), a Selection from the admired engravings which have appeared in the Graphic and a Description of the Art of Wood Engraving with numerous illustrations. *London*, 1876, *folio*

GRATIOT (Amédée). Pétition à MM. les Députés pour qu'ils sauvent l'Imprimerie. *Paris*, 1839, 8vo

GRAVURES de 1468 (Les). Les Armoiries de Charles le Téméraire gravées pour son mariage avec Marguerite d'York. *Liége*, 1877, 16mo

GUICCIARDINI (Lodovico). Descrittione di tutti i Paesi Bassi, altrimenti detti Germania Inferiore. *Anversa*, 1588, *folio 78 plans of cities. The invention of printing is attributed to Haerlem on p. 260*

HANDBOEK ter beoefening der boekdrukkunst in Nederland. *'s Gravenhage*, 1844, 8º

HEINECKEN (C. H. von). Dictionnaire des Artistes dont nous avons des Estampes, avec une notice détaillée de leurs ouvrages gravées. 4 vols. [A— Diz. all that was published]. *Leipsic*, 1778-90, 8º

HUBER (Michael). Origine et progrez de la Gravure. *Berlin*, 1752, 12º

LABUS (Dottore). "Tipografia del Secolo XV." Articolo tratto dalle appendici della Gazzetta Privilegiata di Milano dei giorni 23, 24, 26 Febbraio 1834, num. 34, 35, 37. Con rettificazioni ed aggiunte particolarmente dell' edizioni dai bibliografi non avvertite e scoperte dall' autore dopo la pubblicazione del suo v. vol. intitolato Ricerche Storico-Critiche ec. [by Giacinto Amati]. *Milano*, 1834, 8vo

LEDEBOER (A. M.). Alfabetische Lijst der Boekdrukkers, Boekverkoopers, en Uitgevers in Noord-Nederland sedert de uitvinding van de boekdrukkunst tot den aanvang der negentiende eeuw. *Utrecht*, 1876, 4to *At end:* Drukkersmerken van de van Waesberghen's, met aanwijzing der bladzijden waaraan die ontleend zijn, uit de tweede uitgave van het werk: Het geslacht van Waesberghen

LEIPZIG. Beschreibung aller bei der vierten Säcularfeier der Erfindung der Buchdruckerkunst am 24. 25. und 26. Juni 1840 in Leipzig stattgefundenen Feierlichkeiten. Ein Denkmal für die Mit- und Nachwelt. *Leipzig*, 1840, 8*vo*

LOEDEL (Heinrich). Des Strassburger Malers und Formschneiders Johann Wechtlin, genaant Pilgrim, Holzschnitte in Clair-Obscur in Holz nachgeschnitten. *Leipzig*, 1863, 4°

MARCHIGIAN (Giovanni). Cenni Storici sull' Arte Tipografica. *Lonigo*, 1850, 8*vo*

MEAUME (Edouard). Recherches sur la Vie et les Ouvrages de Jacques Callot, suite au Peintre-Graveur Français de R. Dumesnil. 2 vols. *Nancy*, 1860, 8°

NIÉPCE de ST. VICTOR (Claude). La Gravure héliographique sur acier et sur verre. *Paris*, 1856, 8°

PASSAVANT (Johann David). Le Peintre-Graveur, contenant l'histoire de la Gravure sur bois, sur métal, et au burin jusque vers la fin du 16e Siècle, l'histoire du nielle, &c. 6 vols. *Leipzig*, 1860-64, royal 8°

POUBLON (P. A.). Projet d'un Institut de Gravure à Anvers. *Bruxelles*, 1802, 4°

RAMALEY (David). Employing Printers' Price list for Job Printing. Based on a new plan of measurement, and with detailed prices for all classes of Work. *Saint Paul* [*Minnesota*], 1873, 12*mo*

SCHELLENBERG (Johann Rudolf). Kurze Abhandlung über die Aetzkunst. *Winterthur*, 1795, 8°
Plates

SCHWEGMAN (H.). Het overbrengen von een tekening op een koperen plat. *Harlem*, 1793, 8°

SCHWEGMAN (H.). Verhandeling over het gravuren in de manier von gewassen tekeningen of acquatinta; op twee verschillende wyzen. *Harlem*, 1806, 8°

SILBERMANN (G.). Album d'Impressions Typographiques en Couleur de l'Imprimerie de G. Silbermann à Strasbourg. *Strasbourg*, 1872, 4to

SMITH (Henry). Specimens of Nature Printing from unprepared Plants, etc. etc. *Madras, 1857, folio 99 plates of cereals, ferns and other Indian plants, title printed in gold*

VIENNA. Alfabete des gesammten Erdkreises aus der k. k. Hof-und Staatsdruckerei in Wien. *Wien*, 1876, 4to

INDEX OF PLACES.

Alba
Vernazza

Alost
Holtrop
Iseghem

Altenburg
Dlabacz (Supp.)

America
Fabricius
Jones
Thomas

Amiens
Pouy

Antwerp
Meersch
Ruelens
Ter Bruggen
Willems
Poublon (Supp.)

Augsburg
Herberger
Meyer
Mezger
Panzer
Zapf

Bamberg
Camus
Heller
Jaeck
Laborde
Sprenger

Basle
Geschichte
Stockmeyer

Bavaria
Aretin

Belgium
Burbure
Hoffmann
Iseghem
Lambinet
Meersch
Motteley
Nyenhuis
Vincent
Voisin

Bergamo, Italy
Gallizioli

Berlin
Friedlander
Simon

Bohemia
Ungar
Dlabacz (Supp.)

Bologna
Muzzi

Bordeaux
Gaullier (Supp.)

Bourges
Catherinot

Brescia
Gussago
Lechi
Quirini

Breslau
Fischer
Scheibel

Bretagne
Gauthier
Plaine

Bruges
Carton

Brunswick
Gedenkbuch
Grotefend

Calabria
Capialbi

Catania
Tosto

Chartres
Garnier

Chivasso
Cenno

Cologne
Niesert

Constantinople
Schroenius
Schulze

Cosenza
Lombardi

Côte d'Or
Clement-Janin

Cracow
Bandtkie

Cremona
Bianchi
Rossi

Czenstochow
Siennicki

Dantzic
Schreiber

Dauphiné
Colomb de Batines

Delft
Jacob

Denmark
Hoffmann
Nyrop

Dieppe
Cochet

Dijon
Clement-Janin

Dresden
Flathe
Freyberg
Gottwald

England
Ames
Bowyer
Imbert
Johnson
Lemoine
Middleton
Mores
Palmer
Vertue

Erfurt
Hilaria
Thuringisch

Ferrara
Baruffaldi
Rossi

Finland
Pipping

Florence
Cambiagi
Fantozzi
Fineschi
Moreni
Ottino

Forli
Casali
Zaccaria

France.
Bonnardot
Delandine
Duplessis
Foncemagne
Peignot
Renouvier
Silvestre
Brun (Supp.)
Choffard (Supp.)

Franche Comté
Laire

Frankfort-on-the-Maine
Gedenkbuch

Friuli
Bartolini

Geneva
Gaullieur

Germany
Jubilaum
Renouvier
Semler
Sotheby
Tentzel

Ghent
Vanderhaegen
Voisin

Görlitz
Köhler

Gotha
Engelhard

Gouda
Meersch

Groningen
Oomkens

Guyenne
Delpit (Supp.)

Haarlem
Ampzing
Bowyer
Koning
Koster
Lee
Lehne
Lichtenberger
Linde
Loosjes
Loots
Marnix
Palm
Rapport
Reber
Scheltema
Staveren
Typographia

Halle
Eckstein
Jubelzeugnisse
Schwetschke

Hamburg
Lappenberg

Hanover
Grotefend

Holland
Bradshaw
Carutti
Ebert
Hoffmann
Motteley
Sotheby

Ingoldstadt
Seemiller

Ireland
Folds

Italy
Boni
Coen
Crapelet
Federici
Fumagalli
Hoffmann
Invenzione
Maffei
Ottino
Renouvier
Salvioni
Tosi

Jever
Strackerjan

Königsberg
Geschichte

Leipzig
Flathe
Geschichte
Hasse
Jubilæum
K.
Kade
Leich
Mueller

Liége
Capitaine

Lorraine
Beaupré

Louvain
Even

Lubeck
Seelen

Lusatia
Knauth

Lyons
Pericaud

Magdeburg
Gœtze

Mantua
Volta

Marseilles
Bory

Mayence
Gedenkbuch
Laborde
Marnix
Megerlinus
Wetter
Wurdtwein
Zapf

Mecklenburg
Lisch
Weichmann

Messina
Conferenza
Salvo-Cozzo

Metz
Chabert
Teissier

Milan
Bettoni
Saxe

Mondovi
Danna
Grassi
Vernazza

Mons
Rousselle

Monteleone
Capialbi

Moravia
Elvert

Munster
Niesert

Namur
Capitaine

Naples
Ambra
Giustiniani
Poch

Netherlands
Campbell
Cleef
Eekhoff
Holtrop
Ledeboer
Meerman
Meersch
Nyenhuis
Puy de Montbrun
Rathgeber
Renouvier
Sotheby
Voisin
Westreenen
Handboek (Supp.)

Nördlingen
Beyschlag

Normandy
Frère

Norway and Sweden
Hoffman

Nottinghamshire
Creswell

Nuremburg
Fickenscher
Panzer
Waldau

Ober-Ursel
Kelchner

Oldenburg
Strackerjan

Orleans
Herluison
Polluche

Oxford
Clarendon
Singer

Padua
Sorgato

Palermo
Bozzo
Conferenza
Mira
Pijola
Salvo-Cozzo

Paris
Boutmy
Chevillier
Code
Crapelet
Dibdin
Duprat
Franklin
Gresswell
Guignes
Maittaire
St. Georges
Taillandier

Parma
Affo

Pavia
Comi

Périgord
Fourgeaud (Supp.)

Perugia
Brandolese
Vermiglioli

Piedmont
Brofferio
Vernazza

Poland
Hoffman (J. D.)

Pomerania
Mohnike
Oelrichs

Portugal
Kugelmann
Née

Provence
Henricy

Regensburg
Pangkofer

Reggio
Turri

Ripoli
Fineschi

Rome
Brogiottus
Laire
Quirini

Rouen
Frère

Sabionetta
Rossi

Saint Gallen, Switzerland
Geschichte
Wegelin

Saluzzo
Danna
Gazzera

Salzburg
Suss

Saragossa
Borao

Sardinia
Baille
Spano
Vernazza

Saxony
Freyberg

Sicily
Colosi
Mira
Tornabene

Silesia
Elvert

Spain
Caballero
Mendez
Née

Spires
Bauer

Strasbourg
Invention
Kuntz
Laborde
Lichtenberger
Schmidt

Swabia
Zapf

Sweden
Alnander
Hoffmann
Nachrichten
Schrœder

Switzerland
Gaullieur
Hoffmann
Wegelin

Torgau
Reinhard

Toulouse
Desbarreaux-Bernard
Hubaud

Treviso
Federici

Trino
Clerico

Troyes
Corrard de Breban
Varusoltis

Tubingen
Klemmen
Schnurrer

Turin
Manzoni
Marocco

Turkey
Toderini

Ulm
Hassler

Valencia
Villarroya

Venice
Casali
Morelli
Paetoni
Pellegrini

Verona
Cavattoni
Giuliari

Vicenza
Faccioli

Vienna
Auer
Denis
Kautz
Paris
Schier

Wittenberg
Eichsfeld

Wurtemberg
Schnurrer

York
Davies

Ypres
Diegerick (Supp.)

Zurich
Escher
Ott-Usteri
Rudolph
Vögelin

INDEX OF NAMES OF PRINTERS AND ENGRAVERS.

Aldus, see *Manutius*

Amman
Becker

Audran
Duplessis

Bade
Hoyois

Batelli
Barbera

Bodoni
Bernardi
Jacobacci
Miozzo
Palma
Gamba (Supp.)

Bowyer
Nichols

Bradford
Jones

Breitkopf
Hausius

Brevière
Adeline (Supp.)

Canelles
Spano

Castaldi
Bernardi
Scarabelli

Caxton
Blades
Jones
Knight
Lewis
Middleton
Stephenson

Cennini
Fantozzi
Ottino

Dolet
Boulmier
Née
Picqué

Drevet
Didot

Durer
Scott
Thausing

Ellinger
Heller

Elzevir
Adry
Berard
Dodt van Flensburg
Even
Jacob
Motteley
Pieters
Rammelman
Reume
Walther

Estienne, see *Stephanus*

Froschauer
Rudolph
Vögelin

Fossombrone
Schmid

Franklin
Thayer

Füst
Faccio
Schaab

Ged
Nichols

Gering
Chevillier

Giunta
Bandini

Gutenberg
Dingelstedt
Faccio
Fischer
Fournier
Gama
Gedenkbuch
Geschichte
Invention
Köhler
Laborde
Lamartine
Langenschwarz
Levray
Mahncke
Marlow
Marnix
Meyer
Mueller
Née
Oberlin
Overend
Pallhausen
Pischon
Preusker
Schaab
Scheltema
Schlegel
Schulz
Strasbourg
Winaricky

Henlif
Wetter

Jenson
Sardini

Joris
Molhausen

Koburger
Waldau

Koster
Ampzing
Belinfante
Carutti
Dusseau
Haarlem
Jaager
Koning
Kortebrant
Linde
Loosjes
Marnix
Meurs
Mommaas
Noordziek
Regt
Renouard
Ruelens
Schinkel
Scriverius
Seiz
Staveren
Vries
Weldaad
Westreenen
Zeggelen
Zijll

Lambert
Voisin

Legname
Capialbi

Leeu
Meersch

Luffts
Zeltner

Mansion
Carton
Praet

Manutius
Amoretti
Baschet
Didot
Krause
Manni
Morelli
Nodier
Renouard
Schuck
Sinapius
Unger
Zeno

Marcolini
Casali
Zaccaria

Martens
Gand
Holtrop
Iseghem

Mentel
Dorlan
Niesert

Morin
Frère

Nobili (Gaetano)
Ambra

Nutius
Nuyts

Oporinus
Jociscus

Perna
Manni

Pfister
Camus

Plantin
Hulst
Ruelens
Straelen

Schinkel
Jacob

Schöffer
Dahl
Faccio
Lange
Mueller
Schaab

Senefelder
Nagler

Silvius
Notes

Soncini
Zaccaria

Spira
Denis
Pellegrini

Stephanus
Almeloveen
Bernard
Crapelet
Didot
Gresswell
Maittaire
Renouard

Tory
Bernard

Torrentino
Moreni
Vernazza

Verard
Renouvier

Vitré
Bernard

Volpi
Federici

Vostre
Renouvier

Werrecorren
Even

149

www.ingramcontent.com/pod-product-compliance
Lightning Source LLC
Chambersburg PA
CBHW030340170426
43202CB00010B/1192